Topps BASEBALL CARD BOOKS
are published by

PRICE STERN SLOAN

There is a **Topps** BASEBALL CARD BOOK for every
major league team. Collect them all
or concentrate on your favorites.

Available for all 26 teams!

This library reinforced edition is available exclusively from:

 Grolier Educational Corporation
SHERMAN TURNPIKE, DANBURY, CONNECTICUT 06816

You'll find books for all 26 major league teams at the
Topps BOOKS HEADQUARTERS STORE. To locate
the HEADQUARTERS nearest you, simply call:

PRICE STERN SLOAN
(800) 421-0892
Calling from CA (800) 227-8801

BASEBALL CARDS

Text by

Jim Schultz

PRICE STERN SLOAN

Los Angeles

Published by Price Stern Sloan, Inc.
360 North La Cienega Boulevard, Los Angeles, California 90048

ISBN 0-8431-2468-7

Officially licensed by Major League Baseball

Official Licensee

© 1988 MLBPA
© MSA

An MBKA Production

Printed and bound in Hong Kong.

TEAM LEADERS

Year-by-Year Batting Leaders

Home Runs

1954 - Vern Stephens (8)
1955 - Gus Triandos (12)
1956 - Gus Triandos (21)
1957 - Gus Triandos (19)
1958 - Gus Triandos (30)
1959 - Gus Triandos (25)
1960 - Ron Hansen (22)
1961 - Jim Gentile (46)
1962 - Jim Gentile (33)
1963 - Boog Powell (25)
1964 - Boog Powell (39)
1965 - Curt Blefary (22)
1966 - Frank Robinson (49)
1967 - Frank Robinson (30)
1968 - Brooks Robinson (17)
1969 - Boog Powell (37)
1970 - Boog Powell (35)
1971 - Frank Robinson (28)
1972 - Boog Powell (21)
1973 - Earl Williams (22)
1974 - Bobby Grich (19)
1975 - Don Baylor (25)
1976 - Reggie Jackson (27)
1977 - Lee May
     Eddie Murray (27)
1978 - Doug DeCinces (28)
1979 - Ken Singleton (35)
1980 - Eddie Murray (32)
1981 - Eddie Murray (22)
1982 - Eddie Murray (32)
1983 - Eddie Murray (33)
1984 - Eddie Murray (29)
1985 - Eddie Murray (31)
1986 - Cal Ripken (25)
1987 - Larry Sheets (31)
1988 - Eddie Murray (28)

Runs Batted In

Vern Stephens (46)
Gus Triandos (65)
Gus Triandos (88)
Gus Triandos (72)
Gus Triandos (79)
Gene Woodling (77)
Jim Gentile (98)
Jim Gentile (141)
Jim Gentile (87)
Boog Powell (82)
Brooks Robinson (118)
Brooks Robinson (80)
Frank Robinson (122)
Frank Robinson (94)
Boog Powell (85)
Boog Powell (121)
Boog Powell (114)
Frank Robinson (99)
Boog Powell (81)
Tommy Davis (89)
Tommy Davis (84)
Lee May (99)
Lee May (109)
Lee May
Ken Singleton (99)
Eddie Murray (95)
Ken Singleton (111)
Eddie Murray (116)
Eddie Murray (78)
Eddie Murray (110)
Eddie Murray (111)
Eddie Murray (110)
Eddie Murray (124)
Eddie Murray (84)
Cal Ripken (98)
Eddie Murray (84)

Batting Average

Cal Abrams (.293)
Gus Triandos (.277)
Bob Nieman (.322)
Bob Boyd (.318)
Gene Woodling (.276)
Gene Woodling (.300)
Brooks Robinson (.294)
Jim Gentile (.302)
Brooks Robinson (.303)
Al Smith (.272)
Brooks Robinson (.317)
Brooks Robinson (.297)
Frank Robinson (.316)
Frank Robinson (.311)
Brooks Robinson (.253)
Frank Robinson (.308)
Frank Robinson (.306)
Merv Rettenmund (.318)
Bobby Grich (.278)
Tommy Davis (.306)
Tommy Davis (.289)
Ken Singleton (.300)
Ken Singleton (.278)
Ken Singleton (.328)

Ken Singleton (.293)
Eddie Murray (.295)
Al Bumbry (.318)
Eddie Murray (.294)
Eddie Murray (.316)
Cal Ripken (.318)
Eddie Murray (.306)
Eddie Murray (.297)
Eddie Murray (.305)
Larry Sheets (.316)
Eddie Murray (.284)

Most Valuable Players

1954 - Chuck Diering
1955 - Dave Philley
1956 - Bob Nieman
1957 - Billy Gardner
1958 - Gus Triandos
1959 - Gene Woodling
1960 - Brooks Robinson
1961 - Jim Gentile
1962 - Brooks Robinson
1963 - Stu Miller
1964 - Brooks Robinson
1965 - Stu Miller
1966 - Frank Robinson
1967 - Frank Robinson
1968 - Dave McNally
1969 - Boog Powell
1970 - Boog Powell
1971 - Brooks Robinson
       Frank Robinson
1972 - Jim Palmer
1973 - Jim Palmer
1974 - Paul Blair, Mike Cuellar
1975 - Ken Singleton
1976 - Lee May
1977 - Ken Singleton
1978 - Eddie Murray
1979 - Ken Singleton
1980 - Al Bumbry
1981 - Eddie Murray
1982 - Eddie Murray
1983 - Eddie Murray
       Cal Ripken
1984 - Eddie Murray
1985 - Eddie Murray
1986 - Don Aase
1987 - Larry Sheets

Year-by-Year Pitching Leaders

	Wins	Innings	Earned Run Average
1954	Joe Coleman (13)	Joe Coleman (221)	Duane Pillette (3.12)
1955	Jim Wilson (12)	Jim Wilson (235)	Jim Wilson (3.45)
1956	Ray Moore (12)	Ray Moore (185)	Connie Johnson (3.42)
1957	Connie Johnson (14)	Connie Johnson (242)	Connie Johnson (3.20)
1958	Arnold Portocarrero (15)	Jack Harshman (236)	Jack Harshman (2.90)
1959	Milt Pappas	Hoyt Wilhelm (226)	Hoyt Wilhelm (2.19)
	Hoyt Wilhelm (15)		
1960	Chuck Estrada (18)	Chuck Estrada (209)	Hal "Skinny" Brown (3.06)
1961	Steve Barber (18)	Steve Barber (248)	Milt Pappas (3.03)
1962	Milt Pappas (12)	Chuck Estrada (223)	Robin Roberts (2.78)
1963	Steve Barber (20)	Steve Barber (259)	Steve Barber (2.75)
1964	Wally Bunker (19)	Milt Pappas (252)	Wally Bunker (2.69)
1965	Steve Barber (15)	Steve Barber, Milt Pappas (221)	Milt Pappas (2.61)
1966	Jim Palmer (15)	Dave McNally (213)	Dave McNally (3.17)
1967	Tom Phoebus (14)	Tom Phoebus (208)	Tom Phoebus (3.33)
1968	Dave McNally (22)	Dave McNally (273)	Dave McNally (1.95)
1969	Mike Cuellar (23)	Mike Cuellar (291)	Jim Palmer (2.34)
1970	Mike Cuellar	Jim Palmer (305)	Jim Palmer (2.71)
	Dave McNally (24)		
1971	Dave McNally (21)	Mike Cuellar (292)	Jim Palmer (2.68)
1972	Jim Palmer (21)	Jim Palmer (274)	Jim Palmer (2.07)
1973	Jim Palmer (22)	Jim Palmer (296)	Jim Palmer (2.40)
1974	Mike Cuellar (22)	Ross Grimsley (296)	Ross Grimsley (3.07)
1975	Jim Palmer (23)	Jim Palmer (323)	Jim Palmer (2.09)
1976	Jim Palmer (22)	Jim Palmer (315)	Jim Palmer (2.51)
1977	Jim Palmer (20)	Jim Palmer (319)	Jim Palmer (2.91)
1978	Jim Palmer (21)	Jim Palmer (296)	Jim Palmer (2.46)
1979	Mike Flanagan (23)	Denny Martinez (292)	Mike Flanagan (3.08)
1980	Steve Stone (25)	Scott McGregor (252)	Steve Stone (3.23)
1981	Denny Martinez (14)	Denny Martinez (179)	Sammy Stewart (2.33)
1982	Denny Martinez (16)	Denny Martinez (252)	Jim Palmer (3.13)
1983	Scott McGregor (18)	Scott McGregor (260)	Mike Boddicker (2.77)
1984	Mike Boddicker (20)	Mike Boddicker (261.1)	Mike Boddicker (2.79)
1985	Scott McGregor (14)	Scott McGregor (204)	Ken Dixon (3.67)
1986	Mike Boddicker (14)	Mike Boddicker (218.1)	Mike Flanagan (4.24)
1987	Eric Bell (10)	Mike Boddicker (226)	Mike Boddicker (4.18)
	Mike Boddicker (10)		
	Dave Schmidt (10)		
1988	Jeff Ballard and	Jose Bautista (171.2)	Jose Bautista (4.30)
	Dave Schmidt (8)		

1952

The Browns were the major leagues' most active trading team in Bill Veeck's first full season as owner, and they improved 12 games over their 1951 record to 64-90, but that was good only for seventh place, 31 games behind the Yankees. Outfielder Vic Wertz, obtained from Detroit in an eight-player waiver deal in mid-August, batted .346 in 37 games. Overall, outfielder Bob Nieman (.289, 18 home runs, 74 RBIs) was the offensive leader. Jim Dyck had 15 homers and 64 RBIs while catcher Clint Courtney hit .286 and drove in 50 runs. Bob Cain (12-10, 4.13 ERA) pitched a one-hit, 1-0 win over Cleveland on April 23. Satchel Paige (12-10, 3.07) saved 10 games. Duane Pillette was the other double-figure winner at 10-13. Ned Garver, part of the Aug. 14 trade with the Tigers, was 7-10 with a 3.68 ERA in 21 games for the Browns.

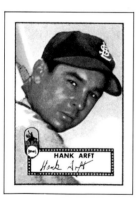

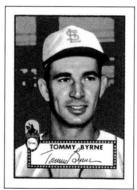

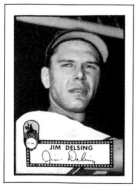

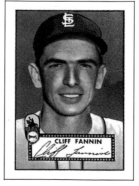

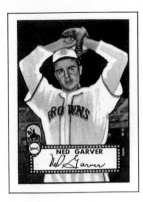

NED GARVER

GORDON GOLDSBERRY

EARL HARRIST

BILL KENNEDY

DICK KRYHOSKI

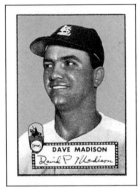

DAVE MADISON

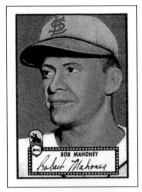

BOB MAHONEY

FRED MARSH

CLARENCE MARSHALL

LES MOSS

DUANE PILLETTE

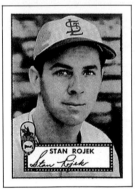

STAN ROJEK

ROY SIEVERS

BOB YOUNG

≡1953≡

The 54-100 Browns, in what turned out to be their last season in St. Louis, fell back into last place, 46½ games behind the dominating Yankees. Vic Wertz, who hit .268, led the team with 19 home runs and 70 RBIs. Outfielder Johnny Groth, acquired from Detroit in the offseason, drove in 57 runs on 10 homers and Dick Kryhoski had 50 in 16 while hitting .278. Reserve outfielder Don Lenhardt actually led the team with a .317 average in 97 games. Roy Sievers, who split time with Kryhoski at first base, batted .270. No pitcher was able to win more than eight games. Reliever Marlin Stuart saved seven games to go with his 8-2 won-lost record. Don Larsen (7-12), Dick Littlefield (7-12) and Duane Pillette (7-13) were the main starters. Satchel Paige recorded 11 saves. The American League approved the sale of the Browns to a group of Baltimore businessmen on Sept. 29 and Jimmy Dykes was hired as manager in November.

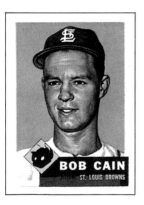
BOB CAIN
pitcher ST. LOUIS BROWNS

Clint COURTNEY
catcher ST. LOUIS BROWNS

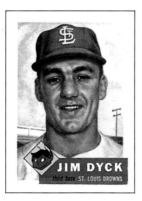
JIM DYCK
third base ST. LOUIS BROWNS

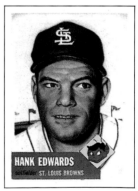
HANK EDWARDS
outfielder ST. LOUIS BROWNS

CLIFF FANNIN
pitcher ST. LOUIS BROWNS

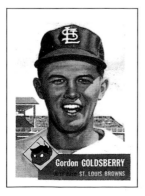
Gordon GOLDSBERRY
first base ST. LOUIS BROWNS

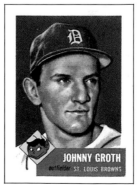
JOHNNY GROTH
outfielder ST. LOUIS BROWNS

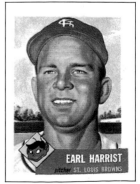
EARL HARRIST
pitcher ST. LOUIS BROWNS

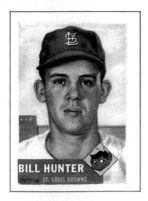

BILL HUNTER
shortstop ST. LOUIS BROWNS

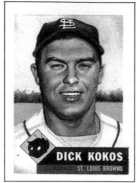

DICK KOKOS
outfielder ST. LOUIS BROWNS

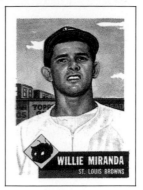

WILLIE MIRANDA
ST. LOUIS BROWNS

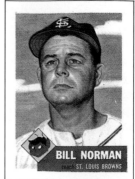

BILL NORMAN
coach ST. LOUIS BROWNS

SATCHELL PAIGE
pitcher ST. LOUIS BROWNS

DUANE PILLETTE
pitcher ST. LOUIS BROWNS

ROY SIEVERS
first base ST. LOUIS BROWNS

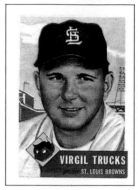

VIRGIL TRUCKS
pitcher ST. LOUIS BROWNS

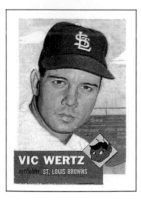

VIC WERTZ
outfielder ST. LOUIS BROWNS

BOB YOUNG
second base ST. LOUIS BROWNS

1954

In their first year in a new city, the Baltimore Orioles drew 1,060,910, about 300,000 more than their best attendance in St. Louis, despite going 54-100 and finishing seventh, 57 games behind the record-setting Cleveland Indians. Bob Turley (14-15, 3.46 ERA) paced the team in wins and the league in strikeouts with 185. Joe Coleman, in a comeback season, was 13-17 with a 3.50 ERA. Duane Pillette (10-14, 3.12) also was effective when he got support. Rightfielder Cal Abrams, obtained from Pittsburgh on May 25, was the team's leading hitter at .293. Co-third basemen Vern Stephens (46 RBIs) and Bob Kennedy (45) provided some power. Stephens batted .285 and first baseman Eddie Waitkus .283. Manager Jimmy Dykes completed the season but White Sox manager Paul Richards was hired in mid-September as the Orioles' manager-general manager. Two months later Richards pulled off the biggest trade in major league history, a deal with the Yankees that involved 18 players.

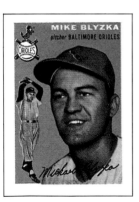

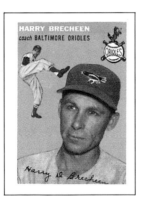

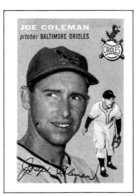

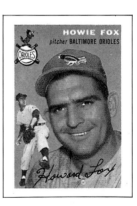

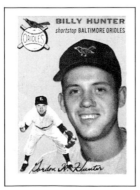

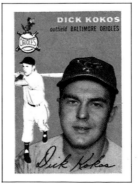

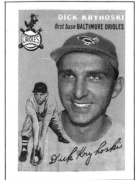

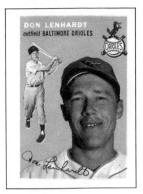

DON LENHARDT
outfield BALTIMORE ORIOLES

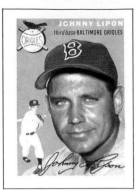

JOHNNY LIPON
third base BALTIMORE ORIOLES

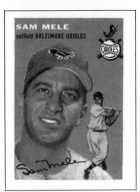

SAM MELE
outfield BALTIMORE ORIOLES

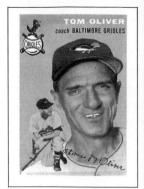

TOM OLIVER
coach BALTIMORE ORIOLES

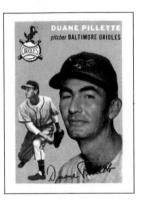

DUANE PILLETTE
pitcher BALTIMORE ORIOLES

VERN STEPHENS
third base BALTIMORE ORIOLES

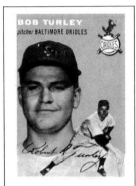

BOB TURLEY
pitcher BALTIMORE ORIOLES

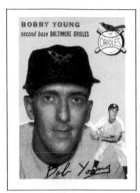

BOBBY YOUNG
second base BALTIMORE ORIOLES

1955

A lack of offense again hurt the Orioles, who wound up 57-97, in seventh place, 39 games behind the Yankees. Paul Richards' club, in last much of the season, passed Washington for seventh by winning four straight from the Senators late in the year and then winning six of their last eight games. The team managed only a .240 batting average, but leftfielder Dave Philley, claimed on waivers from Cleveland on July 2, batted .299 in 82 games. First baseman Gus Triandos, who hit .277, led the team with 12 home runs and 65 RBIs. Rookie Bob Hale, playing behind Triandos, batted .357 in 67 games. Jim Wilson had a 3.45 ERA and won 12 games but he lost 18. Ray Moore was 10-10 with a 3.92 ERA. Richards was active in the trading market, obtaining Harry Dorish (3-3, 3.15, 6 saves) from the White Sox in late June and Bill Wight (6-8, 2.45) from Cleveland in mid-July. Richards also added five "bonus babies" to the roster during the season.

HARRY BRECHEEN coach BALTIMORE ORIOLES

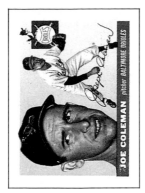

JOE COLEMAN pitcher BALTIMORE ORIOLES

CHUCK DIERING outfield BALTIMORE ORIOLES

DON FERRARESE pitcher BALTIMORE ORIOLES

DON JOHNSON pitcher BALTIMORE ORIOLES

BOB KENNEDY outfield BALTIMORE ORIOLES

FRED MARSH 3rd base BALTIMORE ORIOLES

WILLIE MIRANDA shortstop BALTIMORE ORIOLES

RAY MOORE pitcher BALTIMORE ORIOLES

BILLY O'DELL pitcher BALTIMORE ORIOLES

DUANE PILLETTE pitcher BALTIMORE ORIOLES

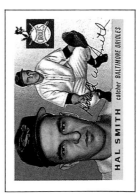

HAL SMITH catcher BALTIMORE ORIOLES

GUS TRIANDOS 1st base BALTIMORE ORIOLES

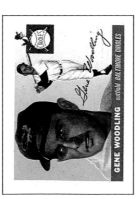

GENE WOODLING outfield BALTIMORE ORIOLES

1956

Outfielder Bob Nieman, third baseman George Kell and pitcher Connie Johnson, acquired from the White Sox on May 21, all helped the Orioles improve 12 games to 69-85 and sixth place, 28 games behind the Yankees. Nieman, the team's lone .300 hitter, batted .322 with 12 home runs and 64 RBIs. Gus Triandos (.279, 2 home runs, 88 RBIs), switched to catcher, again was the power pacesetter. Kell (.261, 8 home runs, 37 RBIs, 102 games) and rightfielder Tito Francona (.258, 9, 57) also contributed offensively. First baseman Bob Boyd batted .311, including a 19-game hitting streak, in 70 games. Ray Moore was the only pitcher to win at least 10 games, going 12-7 with a 4.18 ERA. Johnson (9-10, 3.43), Hal Brown (9-7, 4.03) and Bill Wight (9-12, 4.01) just missed. Reliever George Zuverink led the league with 16 saves and 62 appearances. In the fourth double one-hitter in major league history, Chicago's Hack Harshman beat Johnson and Zuverink, 1-0, June 21.

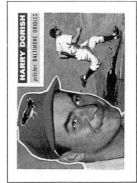

WILLIE MIRANDA
shortstop BALTIMORE ORIOLES

RAY MOORE
pitcher BALTIMORE ORIOLES

BOB NELSON
outfield BALTIMORE ORIOLES

ERV PALICA
pitcher BALTIMORE ORIOLES

DAVE PHILLEY
outfield BALTIMORE ORIOLES

DAVE POPE
outfield BALTIMORE ORIOLES

HAL SMITH
catcher BALTIMORE ORIOLES

GUS TRIANDOS

BILL WIGHT
pitcher BALTIMORE ORIOLES

JIM WILSON
pitcher BALTIMORE ORIOLES

GEORGE ZUVERINK
pitcher BALTIMORE ORIOLES

BALTIMORE ORIOLES

1957

The Orioles continued to show steady improvement. They attained the .500 level, 76-76, for the first time in Baltimore, and finished fifth, 21 games behind the Yankees and just one game behind the fourth-place Tigers. The pitching staff recorded a composite 3.46 ERA, third in the league. George Zuverink, working out of the bullpen, was the low man at 2.47. He was 10-6 with nine saves in a league-high 56 appearances. Unlucky Billy O'Dell, who started and relieved, had a 2.70 ERA but was 4-10. Connie Johnson (14-11, 3.20 ERA), Billy Loes (12-7, 3.25) and Ray Moore (11-13, 3.72) were the big winners. The O's were slightly better offensively, too, as the team batting average climbed to .252. Bob Boyd (.318, 4 home runs, 34 RBIs) and utility man Bill Goodman, who hit .308 in 73 games after being obtained from Boston in mid-June, led the way. Gus Triandos topped the team in homers, 19, and RBIs, 72.

BALTIMORE ORIOLES

BOB Boyd
BALTIMORE ORIOLES 1st BASE

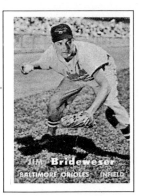

JIM Brideweser
BALTIMORE ORIOLES INFIELD

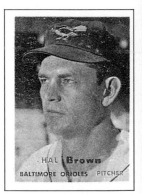

HAL Brown
BALTIMORE ORIOLES PITCHER

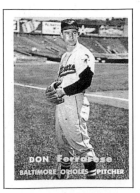

DON Ferrarese
BALTIMORE ORIOLES PITCHER

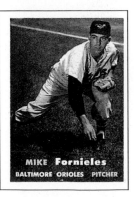

MIKE Fornieles
BALTIMORE ORIOLES PITCHER

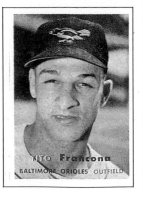

TITO Francona
BALTIMORE ORIOLES OUTFIELD

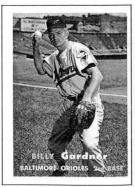

BILLY Gardner
BALTIMORE ORIOLES 2nd BASE

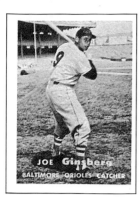

JOE Ginsberg
BALTIMORE ORIOLES CATCHER

BOB Hale
BALTIMORE ORIOLES 1st BASE

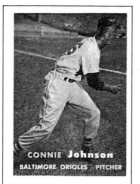

CONNIE Johnson
BALTIMORE ORIOLES PITCHER

GEORGE K
BALTIMORE ORIOLES 3rd BASE

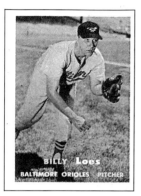

BILLY Loes
BALTIMORE ORIOLES PITCHER

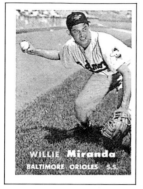

WILLIE Miranda
BALTIMORE ORIOLES S.S.

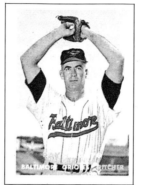

BALTIMORE ORIOLES PITCHER

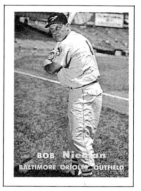

BOB Nieman
BALTIMORE ORIOLES OUTFIELD

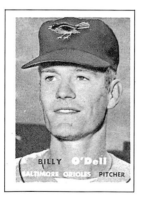

BILLY O'Dell
BALTIMORE ORIOLES PITCHER

BALTIMORE ORIOLES OUTFIELD

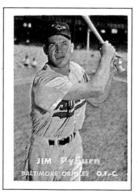

JIM Pyburn
BALTIMORE ORIOLES O.F.C.

BROOKS Robinson
BALTIMORE ORIOLES 3rd B

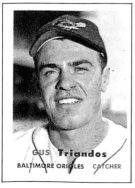

GUS Triandos
BALTIMORE ORIOLES CATCHER

BILL Wight
BALTIMORE ORIOLES PITCHER

DICK Williams
BALTIMORE ORIOLES OUTFIELD

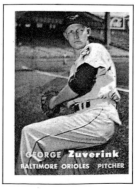

GEORGE Zuverink
BALTIMORE ORIOLES PITCHER

1958

Tied for second place as late as July 27, the Orioles went into an 11-game losing streak which dropped them into sixth and that's where they finished with a 74-79 record, 17½ games behind the Yankees. Once again, the O's relied on pitching, compiling a 3.40 team ERA, second only to New York's. Righthander Arnie Portocarrero (15-11, 3.25 ERA) was acquired from Kansas City on April 17. Young bonus lefty Billy O'Dell (14-11, 2.97 ERA, 8 saves) showed signs of becoming a star. Jack Harshman, obtained from the White Sox during the offseason, was 12-15 with a 2.90 ERA, third in the league, and Milt Pappas went 10-10 in his first full season. Hoyt Wilhelm, claimed on waivers from Cleveland at the beginning of August, pitched a 1-0 no-hitter against the Yankees on Sept. 20. Bob Nieman missed several weeks with an injured hand but still hit .325 with 16 home runs and 60 RBIs. Gus Triandos tied the league record for catchers with 30 homers, Bob Boyd hit .309 and newcomer Gene Woodling batted .276 with 15 homers and 65 RBIs.

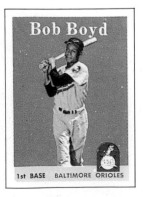

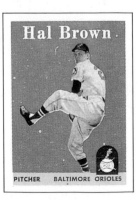

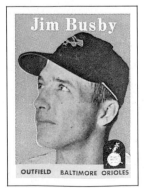

Art Ceccarelli

PITCHER BALTIMORE ORIOLES

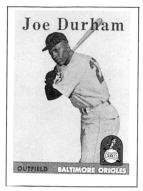

Joe Durham

OUTFIELD BALTIMORE ORIOLES

Billy Gardner

2nd BASE BALTIMORE ORIOLES

Joe Ginsberg

CATCHER BALTIMORE ORIOLES

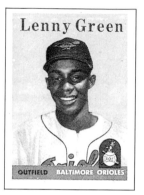

Lenny Green

OUTFIELD BALTIMORE ORIOLES

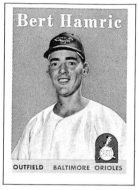

Bert Hamric

OUTFIELD BALTIMORE ORIOLES

Jack Harshman

PITCHER BALTIMORE ORIOLES

Connie Johnson

PITCHER BALTIMORE ORIOLES

George Kell

3rd BASE BALTIMORE ORIOLES

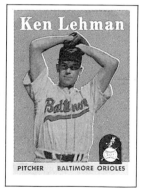

Ken Lehman

PITCHER BALTIMORE ORIOLES

Billy Loes

PITCHER BALTIMORE ORIOLES

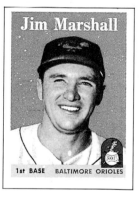

Jim Marshall

1st BASE BALTIMORE ORIOLES

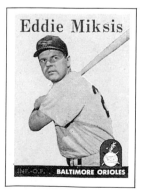

Eddie Miksis

INF.-O.F. BALTIMORE ORIOLES

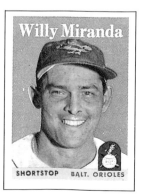

Willy Miranda

SHORTSTOP BALT. ORIOLES

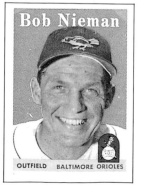

Bob Nieman

OUTFIELD BALTIMORE ORIOLES

Billy O'Dell

PITCHER BALTIMORE ORIOLES

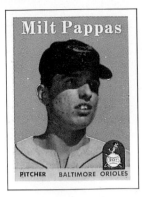

Milt Pappas

PITCHER BALTIMORE ORIOLES

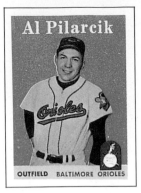

Al Pilarcik

OUTFIELD BALTIMORE ORIOLES

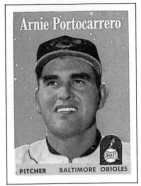

Arnie Portocarrero

PITCHER BALTIMORE ORIOLES

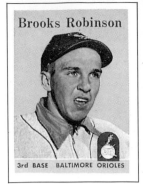

Brooks Robinson

3rd BASE BALTIMORE ORIOLES

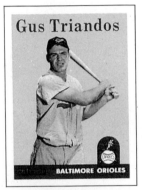

Gus Triandos

BALTIMORE ORIOLES

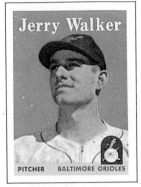

Jerry Walker

PITCHER BALTIMORE ORIOLES

Gene Woodling

BALTIMORE ORIOLES

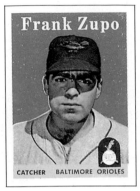

Frank Zupo

CATCHER BALTIMORE ORIOLES

George Zuverink

PITCHER BALTIMORE ORIOLES

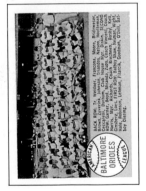

BALTIMORE ORIOLES
AMERICAN LEAGUE

≡1959

Sparked by Hoyt Wilhelm's nearly flawless pitching, the Orioles resided in the first division longer than they had in their Baltimore history. As late as Aug. 26 the O's were in third place. They wound up 74-80, in sixth, 20 games behind the White Sox but only two games in back of the fourth-place Tigers. Wilhelm, who won nis first nine starts before losing to Detroit on June 15, led the league with a 2.19 ERA and finished 15-11. Twenty-year-old Milt Pappas (15-9, 3.27 ERA) hurled four shutouts among his 15 complete games. Jerry Walker (11-10, 2.92 ERA) and Billy O'Dell (10-12, 2.94) also were among the A.L.'s top ten in ERA and helped the Orioles to a 3.56 team mark, second in the league. Hal Brown won 11 games and Billy Loes had 14 saves. Gene Woodling (.300, 14 home runs, 77 RBIs) and Bob Nieman (.292, 21, 60) were the most consistent offensive threats while Gus Triandos led the team with 25 homers and drove in 73 runs.

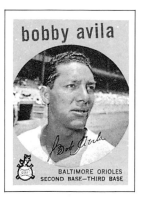

bobby avila

BALTIMORE ORIOLES
SECOND BASE–THIRD BASE

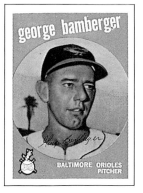

george bamberger

BALTIMORE ORIOLES
PITCHER

charley beamon

BALTIMORE ORIOLES
PITCHER

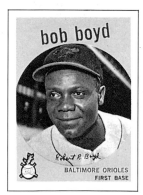

bob boyd

BALTIMORE ORIOLES
FIRST BASE

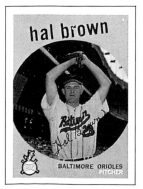

hal brown

BALTIMORE ORIOLES
PITCHER

chico carrasquel

BALTIMORE ORIOLES
SHORTSTOP

jim finigan

BALTIMORE ORIOLES
INFIELD

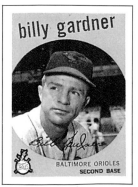

billy gardner

BALTIMORE ORIOLES
SECOND BASE

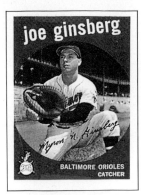

joe ginsberg

BALTIMORE ORIOLES
CATCHER

lenny green

BALTIMORE ORIOLES
OUTFIELD

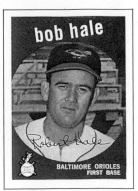

bob hale

BALTIMORE ORIOLES
FIRST BASE

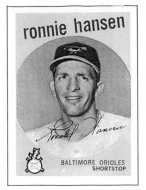

ronnie hansen

BALTIMORE ORIOLES
SHORTSTOP

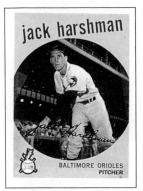

jack harshman

BALTIMORE ORIOLES
PITCHER

connie johnson

BALTIMORE ORIOLES
PITCHER

ernie johnson

BALTIMORE ORIOLES
PITCHER

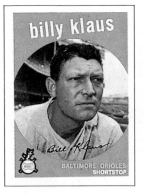

billy klaus

BALTIMORE ORIOLES
SHORTSTOP

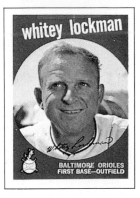

whitey lockman

BALTIMORE ORIOLES
FIRST BASE—OUTFIELD

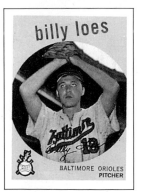

billy loes

BALTIMORE ORIOLES
PITCHER

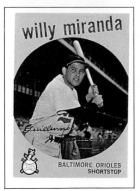

willy miranda

BALTIMORE ORIOLES
SHORTSTOP

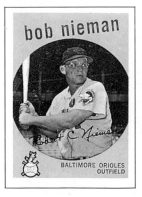

bob nieman

BALTIMORE ORIOLES
OUTFIELD

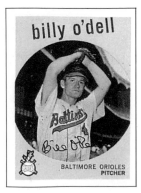

billy o'dell

BALTIMORE ORIOLES
PITCHER

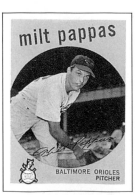

milt pappas

BALTIMORE ORIOLES
PITCHER

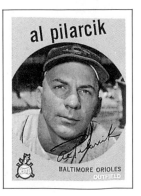

al pilarcik

BALTIMORE ORIOLES
OUTFIELD

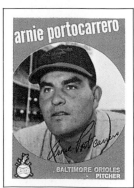

arnie portocarrero

BALTIMORE ORIOLES
PITCHER

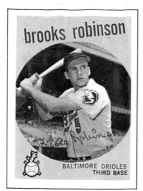

brooks robinson

BALTIMORE ORIOLES
THIRD BASE

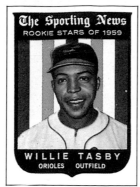

The Sporting News
ROOKIE STARS OF 1959

WILLIE TASBY
ORIOLES OUTFIELD

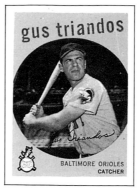

gus triandos

BALTIMORE ORIOLES
CATCHER

The Sporting News

GUS TRIANDOS
CATCHER   AMERICAN LEAGUE
'59 ALL STAR SELECTION

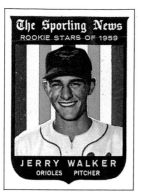

The Sporting News
ROOKIE STARS OF 1959

JERRY WALKER
ORIOLES PITCHER

hoyt wilhelm

BALTIMORE ORIOLES
PITCHER

gene woodling

BALTIMORE ORIOLES
OUTFIELD

george zuverink

BALTIMORE ORIOLES
PITCHER

BALTIMORE Orioles

1960

The Orioles, with five rookies playing regularly, were the surprise team of the league. Picked fifth by most preseason observers, the O's went 89-65 to finish second, eight games behind the Yankees, who won their last 15 games to pull away. The fresh faces included pitchers Chuck Estrada (18-11, 3.57 ERA) and Steve Barber (10-7, 3.21), Rookie of the Year shortstop Ron Hansen (.255, 22 home runs, 86 RBIs), first baseman Jim Gentile (.292, 21, 98) and second baseman Marv Breeding (.267, 3, 43). *The Sporting News* named Estrada, whose 18 wins tied for the league lead, the A.L.'s Pitcher of the Year. Milt Pappas (15-11, 3.36 ERA), Jack Fisher (12-11, 3.41), Hal Brown (12-5, 3.06) and Hoyt Wilhelm (11-8, 3.31, 7 saves) gave the Birds six pitchers with at least 10 wins. Third baseman Brooks Robinson (.294, 14 home runs, 88 RBIs) came into his own and Gene Woodling (.283, 11, 62), Jackie Brandt (.254, 15, 65) and Gus Triandos (.269, 12, 54) lent support.

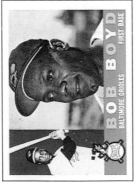
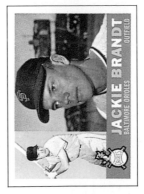

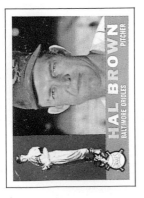

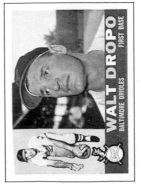

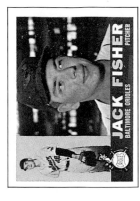

JACK FISHER
PITCHER · BALTIMORE ORIOLES

BILLY GARDNER
SECOND BASE · BALTIMORE ORIOLES

JIM GENTILE
FIRST BASE · BALTIMORE ORIOLES

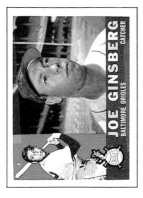

JOE GINSBERG
CATCHER · BALTIMORE ORIOLES

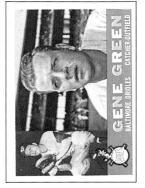

GENE GREEN
CATCHER-OUTFIELD · BALTIMORE ORIOLES

SPORT MAGAZINE
1960 ROOKIE STAR
RONNIE HANSEN
SHORTSTOP · BALT. ORIOLES

BILLY HOEFT
PITCHER · BALTIMORE ORIOLES

GORDON JONES
PITCHER · BALTIMORE ORIOLES

BILLY KLAUS
SHORTSTOP · BALTIMORE ORIOLES

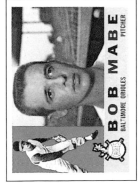

BOB MABE
PITCHER · BALTIMORE ORIOLES

MILT PAPPAS
PITCHER · BALTIMORE ORIOLES

ALBIE PEARSON
OUTFIELD · BALTIMORE ORIOLES

AL PILARCIK
OUTFIELD · BALTIMORE ORIOLES

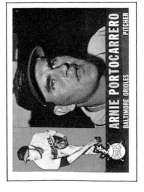

ARNIE PORTOCARRERO
PITCHER · BALTIMORE ORIOLES

JOHNNY POWERS
OUTFIELD · BALTIMORE ORIOLES

ORIOLES
PAUL RICHARDS
MANAGER · BALTIMORE

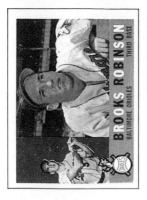

BROOKS ROBINSON
THIRD BASE
BALTIMORE ORIOLES

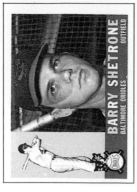

BARRY SHETRONE
OUTFIELD
BALTIMORE ORIOLES

WES STOCK
PITCHER
BALTIMORE ORIOLES

SELECTED BY THE
YOUTH OF AMERICA
WILLIE
TASBY
BALTIMORE ORIOLES
TOPPS ALLSTAR ROOKIE
OUTFIELD

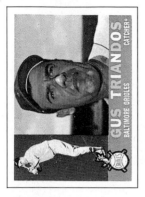

GUS TRIANDOS
CATCHER
BALTIMORE ORIOLES

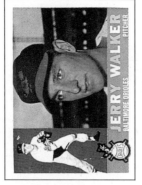

JERRY WALKER
PITCHER
BALTIMORE ORIOLES

HOYT WILHELM
PITCHER
BALTIMORE ORIOLES

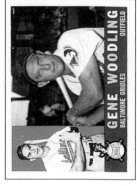

GENE WOODLING
OUTFIELD
BALTIMORE ORIOLES

YOUNG HILL STARS
PAPPAS-FISHER-WALKER

ROBINSON
BRECHEEN
HARRIS
BALTIMORE ORIOLES
COACHES

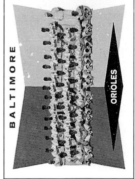

BALTIMORE
ORIOLES

≡1961≡

The Orioles, featuring the slugging of Jim Gentile and the pitching of Steve Barber, improved to 95-67, good for third place, 14 games behind the Yankees in the new 10-team American League. Gentile set an Oriole record with 46 home runs, including a major league standard-tying five grand slams, broke his own club record with 141 RBIs, one behind Roger Maris' league-leading total, and hit .302. Barber (18-12, 3.34 ERA) tied for the league high with eight shutouts. Other starters included Chuck Estrada (15-9, 3.69), Milt Pappas (13-9, 3.03), Hal Brown (10-6, 3.18) and Jack Fisher (10-13, 3.90). Reliable reliever Hoyt Wilhelm (9-7, 2.29 ERA, 18 saves) helped lower the team's league-best ERA to 3.22. Jackie Brandt (.297, 16 home runs, 72 RBIs), Brooks Robinson (.287, 7, 61) and Gus Triandos (.244, 17, 63) were the other big offensive guns. Coach Lum Harris took over as manager for Paul Richards, who stepped aside on Sept. 1 to become the general manager of the new Houston Colt .45s.

JERRY ADAIR
Second Base-Shortstop — Baltimore Orioles

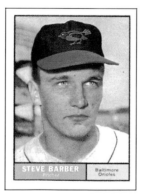

STEVE BARBER
Pitcher — Baltimore Orioles

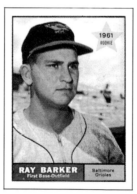

RAY BARKER
First Base-Outfield — Baltimore Orioles

JACKIE BRANDT
Outfield — Baltimore Orioles

MARV BREEDING
Second Base — Baltimore Orioles

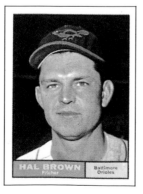

HAL BROWN
Pitcher — Baltimore Orioles

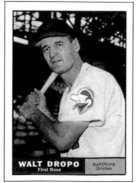

WALT DROPO
First Base — Baltimore Orioles

CHUCK ESTRADA
Pitcher — Baltimore Orioles

JACK FISHER
Pitcher — Baltimore Orioles

JACK FISHER
Pitcher — Baltimore Orioles

HANK FOILES
Catcher — Baltimore Orioles

JIM GENTILE
First Base — Baltimore Orioles

RON HANSEN
Shortstop — Baltimore Orioles

BILLY HOEFT
Pitcher — Baltimore Orioles

GORDON JONES
Pitcher — Baltimore Orioles

DAVE NICHOLSON
Outfield — Baltimore Orioles

MILT PAPPAS
Pitcher — Baltimore Orioles

DAVE PHILLEY
Infield-Outfield — Baltimore Orioles

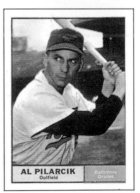

AL PILARCIK
Outfield — Baltimore Orioles

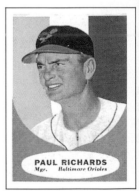

PAUL RICHARDS
Mgr. — Baltimore Orioles

PAUL RICHARDS—MGR.

BROOKS ROBINSON
Third Base — Baltimore Orioles

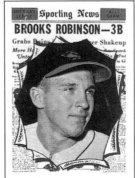

BROOKS ROBINSON—3B

EARL ROBINSON
Outfield — Baltimore Orioles

GENE STEPHENS
Outfield
Baltimore Orioles

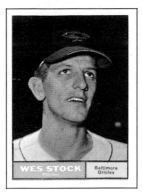

WES STOCK
Pitcher
Baltimore Orioles

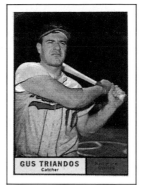

GUS TRIANDOS
Catcher
Baltimore Orioles

JERRY WALKER
Pitcher
Baltimore Orioles

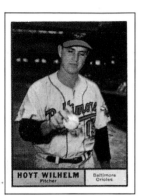

HOYT WILHELM
Pitcher
Baltimore Orioles

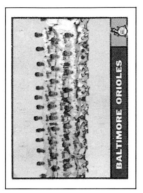

BALTIMORE ORIOLES

1962

New manager Billy Hitchcock couldn't prevent a slide to 77-85 and seventh place, 19 games behind the Yankees. The pitching staff, with a league-best 3.692 ERA, again was the mainstay, even though it lacked a big winner. Robin Roberts (10-9, 2.78 ERA), signed as a free agent on May 21 after being released by the Yankees, showed he could still get the job done. His ERA was second in the league. Milt Pappas (12-10, 4.04 ERA), Steve Barber (9-6, 3.47), Jack Fisher (7-9, 5.09) and Chuck Estrada (9-17, 3.83) all were effective at times. Reliever Hoyt Wilhelm recorded 15 saves while going 7-10 with a 1.94 ERA. A military commitment limited Barber to weekend appearances until mid-June and he missed five weeks late in the season with mononucleosis. Despite a second-half slump, Jim Gentile led the team in home runs, 33, and RBIs, 87. A 19-game hitting streak helped Russ Snyder bat a team-high .305 and Brooks Robinson improved to .303, 23 home runs and 86 RBIs.

JERRY
ADAIR
BALT. ORIOLES   SS

STEVE
BARBER
BALT. ORIOLES   P

JACKIE
BRANDT
BALT. ORIOLES   OF

MARV
BREEDING
BALT. ORIOLES   2B

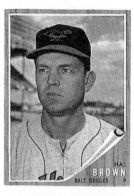

HAL
BROWN
BALT. ORIOLES   P

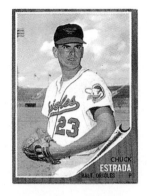

CHUCK
ESTRADA
BALT. ORIOLES   P

JACK
FISHER
BALT. ORIOLES   P

HANK
FOILES
BALT. ORIOLES   C

JIM
GENTILE
BALT. ORIOLES   1B

DICK
HALL
BALT. ORIOLES   P

RON
HANSEN
BALT. ORIOLES   SS

WHITEY
HERZOG
BALT. ORIOLES   OF

BILLY
HITCHCOCK
BALT. ORIOLES   MGR

BILLY
HOEFT
BALT. ORIOLES   P

CHARLEY
LAU
BALT. ORIOLES   C

DAVE
NICHOLSON
BALT. ORIOLES   OF

MILT
PAPPAS
BALT. ORIOLES P

1962 ROOKIE

JOHN
POWELL
BALT. ORIOLES OF

BROOKS
ROBINSON
BALT. ORIOLES 3B

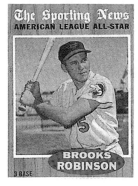

The Sporting News
AMERICAN LEAGUE ALL-STAR

BROOKS
ROBINSON
3 BASE

EARL
ROBINSON
BALT. ORIOLES OF

BILL
SHORT
BALT. ORIOLES P

RUSS
SNYDER
BALT. ORIOLES OF

WES
STOCK
BALT. ORIOLES P

JOHNNY
TEMPLE
BALT. ORIOLES 2B

GUS
TRIANDOS
BALT. ORIOLES C

OZZIE
VIRGIL
BALT. ORIOLES 3B

HOYT
WILHELM
BALT. ORIOLES

DICK
WILLIAMS
ORIOLES OF-INF.

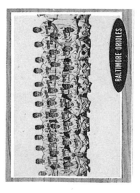

BALTIMORE ORIOLES

1963

Two offseason trades directly influenced the Orioles' climb to 86-76 and fourth place, 18½ games behind the Yankees. Pitcher Stu Miller came from San Francisco and shortstop Luis Aparicio from the White Sox. Miller (5-8, 2.25 ERA), selected Fireman of the Year by *The Sporting News*, led the A.L. in saves with 28 and appearances with 71. Aparicio led the league in stolen bases for the eighth straight year with 40 and helped the O's set a major league record for fewest errors with 99. John Orsino, also included in the Giant trade, took over at catcher and hit .272. Outfielder Boog Powell topped the team with 25 home runs and 82 RBIs. Steve Barber (20-13, 2.75 ERA) became the first 20-game winner in the new Baltimore era, Milt Pappas (16-9, 3.03) enjoyed his finest year and veteran Robin Roberts (14-13, 3.33) had his best season since 1958. Coach Hank Bauer was named in mid-November after Billy Hitchcock had been released on the last day of the season.

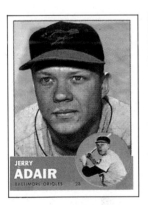

JERRY
ADAIR
BALTIMORE ORIOLES   2B

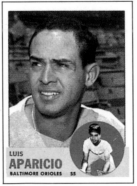

LUIS
APARICIO
BALTIMORE ORIOLES   SS

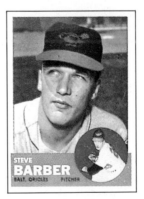

STEVE
BARBER
BALT. ORIOLES   PITCHER

JACKIE
BRANDT
BALT. ORIOLES   OF

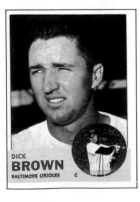

DICK
BROWN
BALTIMORE ORIOLES   C

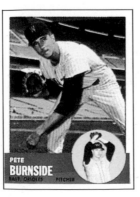

PETE
BURNSIDE
BALT. ORIOLES   PITCHER

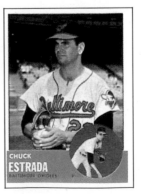

CHUCK
ESTRADA
BALTIMORE ORIOLES

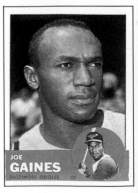

JOE
GAINES
BALTIMORE ORIOLES   OF

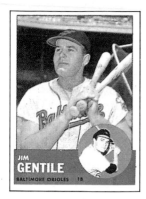

JIM
GENTILE
BALTIMORE ORIOLES 1B

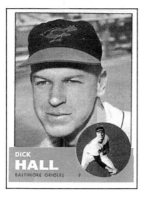

DICK
HALL
BALTIMORE ORIOLES P

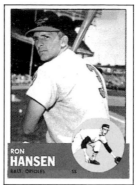

RON
HANSEN
BALT. ORIOLES SS

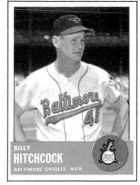

BILLY
HITCHCOCK
BALTIMORE ORIOLES MGR.

BOB
JOHNSON
BALT. ORIOLES INF-OF

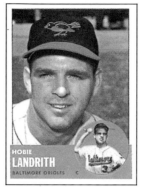

HOBIE
LANDRITH
BALTIMORE ORIOLES C

CHARLIE
LAU
BALT. ORIOLES CATCHER

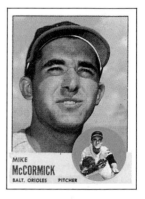

MIKE
McCORMICK
BALT. ORIOLES PITCHER

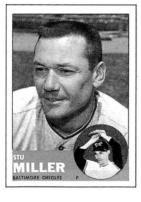

STU
MILLER
BALTIMORE ORIOLES P

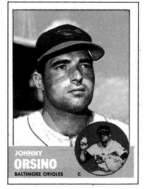

JOHNNY
ORSINO
BALTIMORE ORIOLES C

MILT
PAPPAS

BOOG
POWELL
BALTIMORE ORIOLES OF

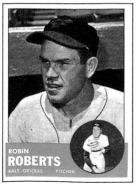

ROBIN
ROBERTS
BALT. ORIOLES PITCHER

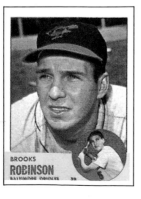

BROOKS
ROBINSON
BALTIMORE ORIOLES 3B

RUSS
SNYDER
BALTIMORE ORIOLES OF

WES
STOCK
BALTIMORE ORIOLES

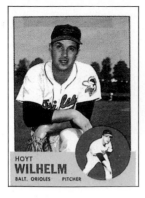

HOYT
WILHELM
BALT. ORIOLES   PITCHER

BALTIMORE ORIOLES

1964

The Orioles were in first place more days, 84, than either the champion Yankees or the second-place White Sox but eventually finished third, two games out of the top spot and one game behind Chicago. Their 97-65 record was their best in Baltimore. Brooks Robinson led the league with 118 RBIs, was second in batting average at .317 and hit 28 home runs to win the A.L. Most Valuable Player award in a landslide. Boog Powell was second in the league with 39 homers, first in slugging percentage at .606, drove in 99 runs and hit .290. Luis Aparicio led the league for the ninth straight year with a career-high 57 stolen bases and helped lower the team's own major league record for fewest errors to 95. Wally Bunker, 19, earned Rookie Pitcher of the Year honors from *The Sporting News* by going 19-5 with a 2.69 ERA. Milt Pappas (16-7, 2.96 ERA) pitched seven shutouts. Robin Roberts (13-7, 2.91 ERA) was effective and Stu Miller again anchored the bullpen with 23 saves. The team ERA fell to 3.16.

ORIOLES

JERRY ADAIR   2nd base

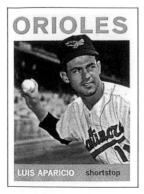

ORIOLES

LUIS APARICIO   shortstop

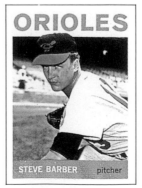

ORIOLES

STEVE BARBER   pitcher

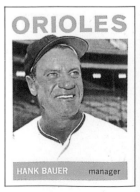

ORIOLES

HANK BAUER   manager

ORIOLES
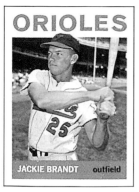
JACKIE BRANDT outfield

ORIOLES

GEORGE BRUNET pitcher

ORIOLES
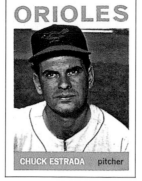
CHUCK ESTRADA pitcher

ORIOLES
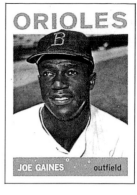
JOE GAINES outfield

ORIOLES

HARVEY HADDIX pitcher

ORIOLES
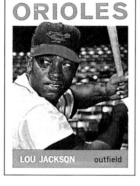
LOU JACKSON outfield

ORIOLES
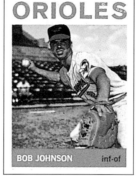
BOB JOHNSON inf-of

ORIOLES

WILLIE KIRKLAND outfield

ORIOLES
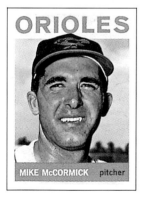
MIKE McCORMICK pitcher

ORIOLES
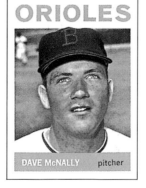
DAVE McNALLY pitcher

ORIOLES

STU MILLER pitcher

ORIOLES
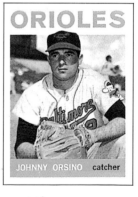
JOHNNY ORSINO catcher

ORIOLES

MILT PAPPAS pitcher

ORIOLES
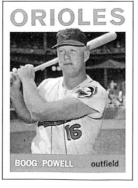
BOOG POWELL outfield

ORIOLES

ROBIN ROBERTS pitcher

ORIOLES

BROOKS ROBINSON 3b

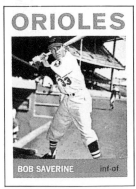

ORIOLES

BOB SAVERINE   inf-of

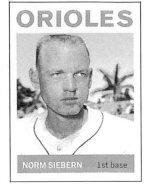

ORIOLES

NORM SIEBERN   1st base

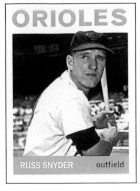

ORIOLES

RUSS SNYDER   outfield

ORIOLES

HERM STARRETTE   pitcher

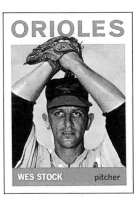

ORIOLES

WES STOCK   pitcher

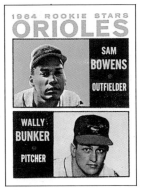

1964 ROOKIE STARS
ORIOLES

SAM BOWENS   OUTFIELDER

WALLY BUNKER   PITCHER

1964 ROOKIE STARS
ORIOLES

DAROLD KNOWLES   PITCHER

LES NARUM   PITCHER

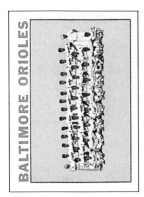

BALTIMORE ORIOLES

1965

In the thick of the pennant race for the first half of the season, the Orioles wound up 94-68, in third place, eight games behind Minnesota and one game in back of the second-place White Sox. Brooks Robinson, bothered early by injuries, came on strong during the team's August slump to lead the club with 80 RBIs and a .297 batting average. Leftfielder Curt Blefary, the A.L. Rookie of the Year, led the team with 22 home runs and had 70 RBIs. By now good pitching was becoming synonymous with the Orioles. Their 2.98 ERA was the best in the league and six hurlers won at least 10 games. There were few weak links among Steve Barber (15-10, 2.69 ERA), Milt Pappas (13-9, 2.61), Dave McNally (11-6, 2.85), Wally Bunker (10-8, 3.38) and relievers Stu Miller (14-7, 1.89, 24 saves) and Dick Hall (11-8, 3.06, 12 saves). In December the Orioles traded three players to the Reds for Frank Robinson.

ORIOLES

2nd BASE

JERRY ADAIR

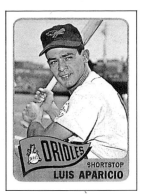

ORIOLES

SHORTSTOP

LUIS APARICIO

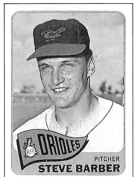

ORIOLES

PITCHER

STEVE BARBER

ORIOLES

MANAGER

HANK BAUER

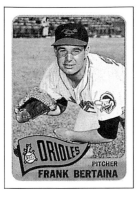

ORIOLES

PITCHER

FRANK BERTAINA

ORIOLES

OUTFIELD

SAM BOWENS

ORIOLES

OUTFIELD

JACKIE BRANDT

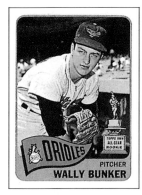

ORIOLES

PITCHER

WALLY BUNKER

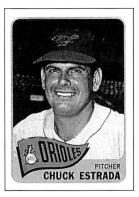

ORIOLES

PITCHER

CHUCK ESTRADA

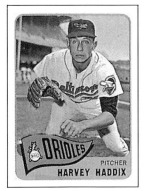

ORIOLES

PITCHER

HARVEY HADDIX

ORIOLES

INF-OUTFIELD

BOB JOHNSON

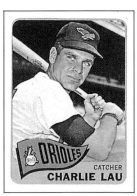

ORIOLES

CATCHER

CHARLIE LAU

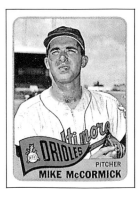

ORIOLES

PITCHER

MIKE McCORMICK

ORIOLES

PITCHER

DAVE McNALLY

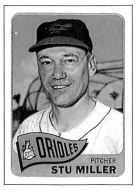

ORIOLES

PITCHER

STU MILLER

ORIOLES

CATCHER

JOHNNY ORSINO

PITCHER
MILT PAPPAS

OUTFIELD
BOOG POWELL

PITCHER
ROBIN ROBERTS

3rd BASE
BROOKS ROBINSON

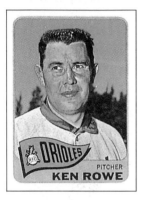

PITCHER
KEN ROWE

INF-OF
BOB SAVERINE

1ST BASE
NORM SIEBERN

OUTFIELD
RUSS SNYDER

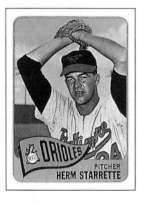

PITCHER
HERM STARRETTE

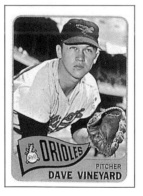

PITCHER
DAVE VINEYARD

1965 ROOKIE STARS
DAVE JOHNSON 2b-ss
PAUL BLAIR outfield

1965 ROOKIE STARS
JOHN MILLER pitcher
CURT BLEFARY 1st b-of

3RD PLACE - AMERICAN LEAGUE

1966

Frank Robinson proved that one man could make the difference between an also-ran and a World Champion. The veteran outfielder became the first man to win Most Valuable Player honors in both leagues (having won the award while with Cincinnati in 1961) and the 10th major leaguer in history to win the triple crown. The 97-63 Orioles won the A.L. pennant by nine games over Minnesota and swept the Dodgers in four straight games in the World Series. Robinson batted .316, drove in 122 runs and led the majors with a career-high 49 homers. Boog Powell (.287, 34 homers, 109 RBIs), Brooks Robinson (.269, 23, 100) and Curt Blefary (.255, 23, 64) also swung big bats. The relief corps of Stu Miller (18 saves), Eddie Fisher (13 after being acquired from the White Sox June 12), Dick Hall (7) and Moe Drabowsky (5) was called upon often. Jim Palmer won 15 games, Dave McNally 13 and Steve Barber and Wally Bunker 10 each. The O's upset the Dodgers in the World Series by shutting them out in the last three games.

JERRY ADAIR 2nd base

LUIS APARICIO shortstop

STEVE BARBER pitcher

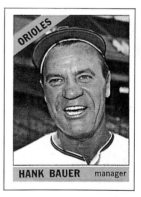

HANK BAUER manager

PAUL BLAIR outfield

CURT BLEFARY outfield

SAM BOWENS outfield

WALLY BUNKER pitcher

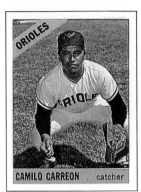

CAMILO CARREON   catcher

MOE DRABOWSKY   pitcher

WOODY HELD   outfield

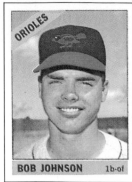

BOB JOHNSON   1b-of

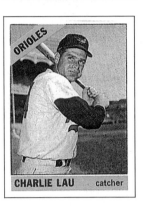

CHARLIE LAU   catcher

DAVE McNALLY   pitcher

JOHN MILLER   pitcher

STU MILLER   pitcher

JIM PALMER   pitcher

MILT PAPPAS   pitcher

BOOG POWELL   outfield

BROOKS ROBINSON   3rd base

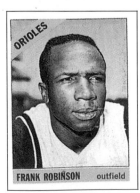

FRANK ROBINSON   outfield

VIC ROZNOVSKY   catcher

NORM SIEBERN   1st base

RUSS SNYDER   outfield

CARL WARWICK outfield

1966 ROOKIE STARS
ANDY ETCHEBARREN c
DAROLD KNOWLES p
ORIOLES

1966 ROOKIE STARS
EDDIE WATT pitcher
ED BARNOWSKI pitcher
ORIOLES

1966 ROOKIE STARS
DAVE JOHNSON
GENE BRABENDER
FRANK BERTAINA
ORIOLES

ORIOLES — 3RD PLACE · AMERICAN LEAGUE

1967

The offense failed to live up to its 1966 performance and the Orioles had to win 12 of their last 16 games to finish 76-85, in sixth place, 15½ games behind Boston. Dependable Frank Robinson missed a month with a concussion and still led the team with 30 home runs, 94 RBIs and a .311 batting average. Centerfielder Paul Blair, showing consistent improvement, hit .293 and led the league in triples with 12. Curt Blefary had 81 RBIs and hit three of his 22 homers in a 16-4 win over the Angels on June 6. Brooks Robinson (.269, 22 homers, 77 RBIs) again fielded marvelously. The team ERA was a respectable 3.32 but Tom Phoebus (14-9, 3.33 ERA), chosen Rookie Pitcher of the Year by *The Sporting News*, was the club's lone double-digit winner. Moe Drabowsky was the most effective reliever with 12 saves and a 1.61 ERA in 43 appearances. Jim Hardin, recalled in June, was 8-3 with a 2.27 ERA. Dave McNally (7-7, 4.54) and Jim Palmer (3-1, 2.94) spent time on the disabled list.

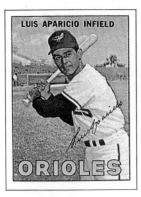

LUIS APARICIO INFIELD

ORIOLES

STEVE BARBER PITCHER

ORIOLES

HANK BAUER · MGR.

ORIOLES

BALL: 1
L.A.: 0

BLAIR'S HOMER DEFEATS L.A.

WORLD SERIES GAME #3

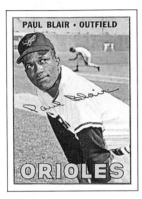

PAUL BLAIR · OUTFIELD

ORIOLES

CURT BLEFARY · OF

ORIOLES

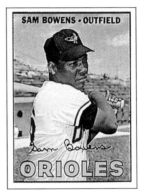

SAM BOWENS · OUTFIELD

ORIOLES

GENE BRABENDER PITCHER

ORIOLES

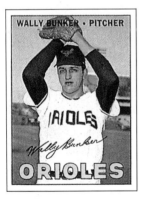

WALLY BUNKER · PITCHER

ORIOLES

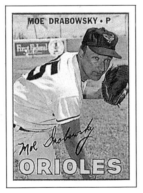

MOE DRABOWSKY · P

ORIOLES

BALL: 5
L.A.: 2

MOE MOWS DOWN 11

WORLD SERIES GAME #1

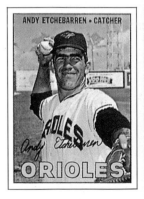

ANDY ETCHEBARREN · CATCHER

ORIOLES

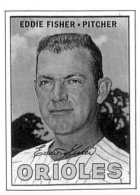

EDDIE FISHER · PITCHER

ORIOLES

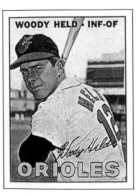

WOODY HELD · INF-OF

ORIOLES

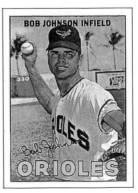

BOB JOHNSON INFIELD

ORIOLES

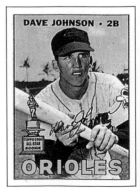

DAVE JOHNSON · 2B

ORIOLES

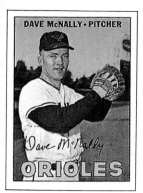

DAVE McNALLY • PITCHER

ORIOLES

CHARLIE LAU • CATCHER

ORIOLES

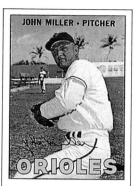

JOHN MILLER • PITCHER

ORIOLES

STU MILLER • PITCHER

ORIOLES

WORLD SERIES GAME #2 — PALMER BLANKS DODGERS

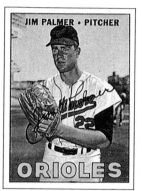

JIM PALMER • PITCHER

ORIOLES

BOOG POWELL • 1B

ORIOLES

BROOKS ROBINSON • 3B

ORIOLES

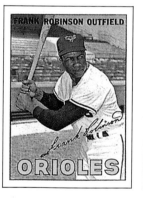

FRANK ROBINSON OUTFIELD

ORIOLES

VIC ROZNOVSKY • C

ORIOLES

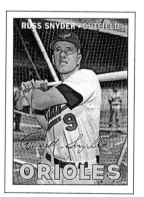

RUSS SNYDER • OUTFIELD

ORIOLES

EDDIE WATT • PITCHER

ORIOLES

BOOG POWELL • CURT BLEFARY

BIRD BOMBERS

F. ROBINSON • H. BAUER • B. ROBINSON — THE CHAMPS

ORIOLES 1967 ROOKIE STARS

LARRY HANEY • C

ED BARNOWSKI • P

ORIOLES

BILL DILLMAN • P

MARK BELANGER • SS-2B

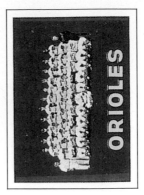

1968

As the pitching improved, so did the Orioles. Both the starters and relievers were consistent throughout the season and the O's rallied under Earl Weaver, who replaced Hank Bauer as manager at the All-Star break, to 91-71. That was good only for second place, 12 games behind Detroit, however, as the Tigers settled a close race in early September. Dave McNally, 8-8 at midseason, won 12 straight to go 22-10 with a 1.95 ERA and 18 complete games. Jim Hardin (18-13, 2.51 ERA) and Tom Phoebus (15-15, 2.61), who no-hit Boston, 6-0, April 27, were also among the league leaders in ERA. Eddie Watt (5-5, 2.28 ERA, 11 saves), Moe Drabowsky (4-4, 1.92, 7 saves) and Pete Richert (6-3, 3.48, 6 saves) all did a good job out of the bullpen as the staff ERA dropped to a club-record 2.66. Boog Powell led the team with 22 homers and 85 RBIs. Don Buford, who played more under Weaver, batted .282, hit 15 homers and stole 27 bases. Weaver, 37 when he took over, was the youngest manager in the league.

HANK BAUER

MARK BELANGER

PAUL BLAIR

CURT BLEFARY

SAM
BOWENS
OUTFIELD ORIOLES

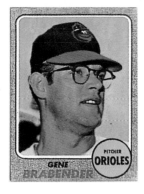

GENE
BRABENDER
PITCHER ORIOLES

DON
BUFORD
2B-3B ORIOLES

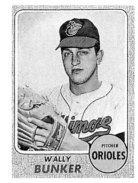

WALLY
BUNKER
PITCHER ORIOLES

BILL
DILLMAN
PITCHER ORIOLES

MOE
DRABOWSKY
PITCHER ORIOLES

ANDY
ETCHEBARREN
CATCHER ORIOLES

LARRY
HANEY
CATCHER ORIOLES

JIM
HARDIN
PITCHER ORIOLES

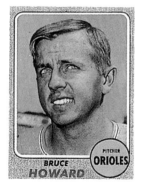

BRUCE
HOWARD
PITCHER ORIOLES

DAVE
JOHNSON
2nd BASE ORIOLES

DAVE
McNALLY
PITCHER ORIOLES

JOHN
O'DONOGHUE
PITCHER ORIOLES

JIM
PALMER
PITCHER ORIOLES

TOM
PHOEBUS
PITCHER ORIOLES

BOOG
POWELL
1st BASE ORIOLES

PITCHER
ORIOLES

PETE
RICHERT

3rd BASE
ORIOLES

BROOKS
ROBINSON

The Sporting News

ALL STAR SELECTION

BROOKS ROBINSON
AMERICAN LEAGUE
THIRD BASE

The Sporting News

ALL STAR SELECTION

FRANK ROBINSON
AMERICAN LEAGUE
OUTFIELDER

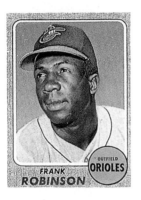

OUTFIELD
ORIOLES

FRANK
ROBINSON

CATCHER
ORIOLES

VIC
ROZNOVSKY

PITCHER
ORIOLES

EDDIE
WATT

1968 ROOKIE STARS

ORIOLES

DAVE MAY • OF

DAVE LEONHARD • P

1968 ROOKIE STARS

ORIOLES

ROGER NELSON • P

CURT MOTTON • OF

1968 ROOKIE STARS

ORIOLES

RON STONE • OF

FRANK PETERS • INF

ORIOLES

AMERICAN LEAGUE

1969

In the first year of divisional play the Orioles broke the American League East race open early, clinching the pennant on Sept. 13 with 17 games left. They went 109-53 and their 19-game bulge over defending World Champion Detroit was the second largest in league history. The O's swept the Twins, the A.L. West kingpins, three straight in the playoffs but, after winning the first contest, lost the World Series to the Mets in five games. Mike Cuellar (23-11, 2.38 ERA), acquired from Houston in the offseason, spearheaded a solid pitching staff. His 23 wins were a team record and he shared the Cy Young Award with Denny McLain. Dave McNally (20-7, 3.21) won a league record-trying 15 consecutive games at the start of the season. Jim Palmer (16-4, 2.34), who missed all of 1968 and 42 days this year with back problems, no-hit Oakland, 8-0, Aug. 13, four days after he came off the disabled list. Tom Phoebus went 14-7 with a 3.52 ERA. Offensively, Boog Powell (.304, 37 home runs, 121 RBIs) and Frank Robinson (.308, 32, 100) were the top guns.

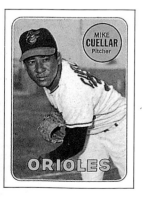

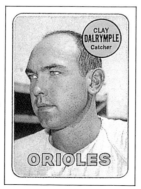

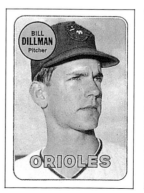

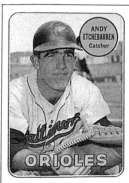

JIM HARDIN
Pitcher

ORIOLES

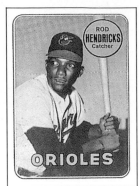

ROD HENDRICKS
Catcher

ORIOLES

DAVE JOHNSON
2nd Base

ORIOLES

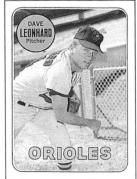

DAVE LEONHARD
Pitcher

ORIOLES

DAVE MAY
Outfield

ORIOLES

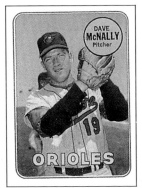

DAVE McNALLY
Pitcher

ORIOLES

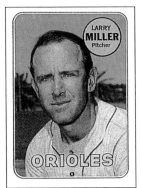

LARRY MILLER
Pitcher

ORIOLES

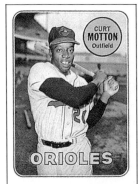

CURT MOTTON
Outfield

ORIOLES

JIM PALMER
Pitcher

ORIOLES

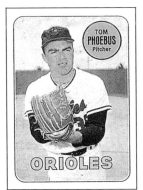

TOM PHOEBUS
Pitcher

ORIOLES

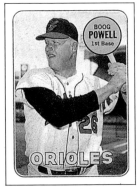

BOOG POWELL
1st Base

ORIOLES

PETE RICHERT
Pitcher

ORIOLES

BROOKS ROBINSON
3rd Base

ORIOLES

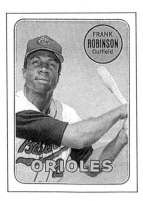

FRANK ROBINSON
Outfield

ORIOLES

The Sporting News

BROOKS ROBINSON
3rd Base
ORIOLES

AMERICAN LEAGUE ALL-STARS

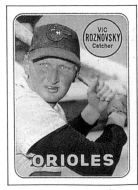

VIC ROZNOVSKY
Catcher

ORIOLES

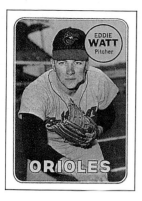

1970

The Orioles carried their 1969 success one step further, beating Cincinnati, 4-1, in the World Series after eliminating the West champion Twins in three straight playoff games. Winning a record 40 one-run games, the O's were 108-54 in the regular season, beating the Yankees by 15 games. Mike Cuellar (24-8, 3.47 ERA), Dave McNally (24-9, 3.22) and Jim Palmer (20-10, 2.71) were baseball's winningest threesome since World War II. Cuellar hurled 21 complete games, McNally won at least 20 for the third straight year, and Palmer's ERA was the second lowest in the league. Boog Powell earned league Most Valuable Player honors with 35 home runs, 114 RBIs and a .297 average. Frank Robinson (.306, 25 homers, 78 RBIs) had another outstanding year, Brooks Robinson drove in 94 runs, reserve outfielder Merv Rettenmund actually led the club in hitting at .322 and Don Buford (.272, 17, 66, 99 runs, 109 walks, 16 stolen bases) again was an invaluable leadoff hitter.

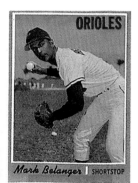
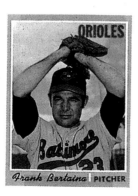

Mike Cuellar | PITCHER

Clayton Dalrymple | C

Andy Etchebarren | CATCHER

Bobby Floyd | SHORTSTOP

Dick Hall | PITCHER

Jim Hardin | PITCHER

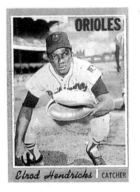

Elrod Hendricks | CATCHER

Dave Johnson | 2ND BASE

Dave Leonhard | PITCHER

Marcelino Lopez | PITCHER

Dave May | OUTFIELD

Dave McNally | PITCHER

Curt Motton | OUTFIELD

Jim Palmer | PITCHER

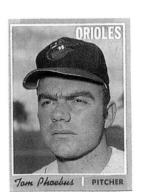

Tom Phoebus | PITCHER

Boog Powell | 1ST BASE

The Sporting News
BOOG POWELL—1B

ORIOLES

Merv Rettenmund OUTFIELD

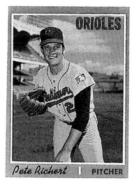

ORIOLES

Pete Richert PITCHER

ORIOLES

Brooks Robinson 3RD BASE

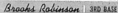

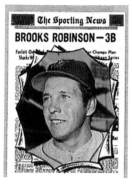

The Sporting News
BROOKS ROBINSON—3B

The Sporting News
FRANK ROBINSON—OF

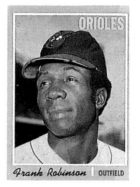

ORIOLES

Frank Robinson OUTFIELD

ORIOLES

Chico Salmon INFIELD

ORIOLES

Tom Shopay OUTFIELD

ORIOLES

Eddie Watt PITCHER

ORIOLES

Earl Weaver MANAGER

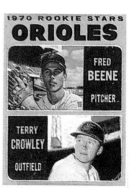

1970 ROOKIE STARS
ORIOLES

FRED BEENE PITCHER

TERRY CROWLEY OUTFIELD

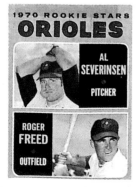

1970 ROOKIE STARS
ORIOLES

AL SEVERINSEN PITCHER

ROGER FREED OUTFIELD

ORIOLES WIN A SQUEEKER!

A.L. PLAYOFF GAME 1

POWELL SCORES WINNING RUN!

A.L. PLAYOFF GAME 2

BIRDS WRAP IT UP!

A.L. PLAYOFF GAME 3

POWELL 26

BUFORD BELTS LEADOFF HOMER!

1971

The Orioles increased their trio of 20-game winners to a quartet and won their third straight American League pennant before losing the World Series in seven games to the Pirates. The O's, 101-57, were 12 games in front of Detroit at the end of the regular season and then eliminated Oakland in three straight playoff games. Dave McNally (21-5, 2.89 ERA), Pat Dobson (20-8, 2.90), Jim Palmer (20-9, 2.68) and Mike Cuellar (20-9, 3.08) — a combined 50 games above .500 — made the Orioles the first team to have four 20-game winners since the 1920 White Sox. The 2.99 team ERA was the best in the A.L. for the third year in a row. Frank Robinson (.281, 28 home runs, a team-high 99 RBIs) hit his 500th career homer on Sept. 13. Boog Powell (.256, 22 homers, 92 RBIs) and Brooks Robinson (.272, 20, 92) supplied additional power, leadoff man Don Buford led the league with 99 runs and Merv Rettenmund hit .319. By winning their last 11 games, the Orioles became only the third team in major league history to win at least 100 games three straight years.

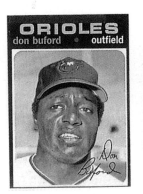

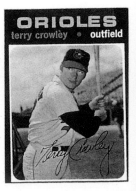

ORIOLES mike cuellar · pitcher

ORIOLES clay dalrymple · catcher
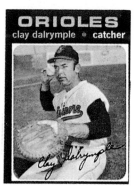

ORIOLES pat dobson · pitcher
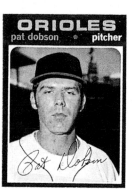

ORIOLES andy etchebarren · c
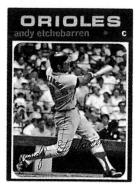

ORIOLES bob grich · shortstop

ORIOLES dick hall · pitcher

ORIOLES jim hardin · pitcher
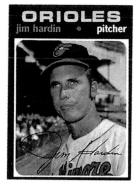

ORIOLES elrod hendricks · catcher
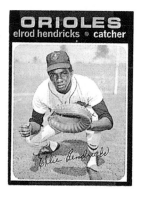

ORIOLES grant jackson · pitcher
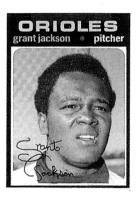

ORIOLES dave johnson · 2nd base

ORIOLES dave leonhard · pitcher

ORIOLES marcelino lopez · pitcher

ORIOLES dave mc nally · pitcher

ORIOLES curt motton · outfield
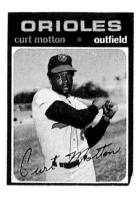

ORIOLES jim palmer · pitcher

ORIOLES boog powell · 1st base

ORIOLES
merv rettenmund • of

ORIOLES
pete richert • pitcher

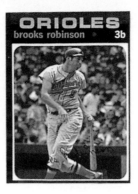

ORIOLES
brooks robinson 3b

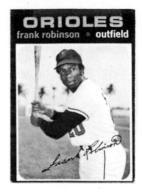

ORIOLES
frank robinson • outfield

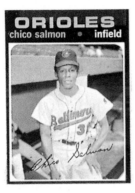

ORIOLES
chico salmon • infield

ORIOLES
eddie watt • pitcher

ORIOLES
earl weaver • manager

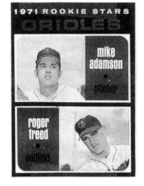

1971 ROOKIE STARS
ORIOLES
mike adamson • pitcher
roger freed • outfield

1970 / GAME #1 A.L. PLAYOFFS — POWELL MUSCLES TWINS!

1970 GAME #2 A.L. PLAYOFFS — McNALLY MAKES IT TWO STRAIGHT!

1970 GAME #3 A.L. PLAYOFFS — PALMER MOWS 'EM DOWN!

1970 / A.L. PLAYOFFS ORIOLES CELEBRATE! — A TEAM EFFORT!

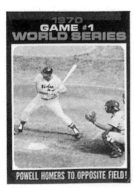

1970 GAME #1 WORLD SERIES — POWELL HOMERS TO OPPOSITE FIELD!

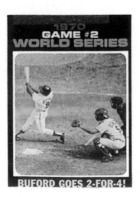

1970 GAME #2 WORLD SERIES — BUFORD GOES 2-FOR-4!

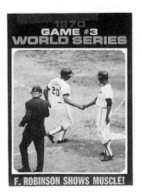

1970 GAME #3 WORLD SERIES — F. ROBINSON SHOWS MUSCLE!

1970 GAME #4 WORLD SERIES — REDS STAY ALIVE!

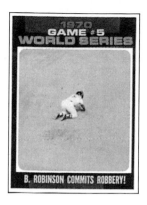

1970 GAME #5 WORLD SERIES

B. ROBINSON COMMITS ROBBERY!

1970/WORLD SERIES CELEBRATION!

CONVINCING PERFORMANCE!

1972

Despite a lack of offense, the Orioles were involved in a pennant race with Detroit, Boston and New York until mid-September and weren't eliminated until a loss to the Red Sox on Sept. 29. The 80-74 O's finished third, five games behind the Tigers in a season delayed at the start by a players' strike. The pitching, as exemplified by a major league-leading 2.53 ERA, once again was superb. The offense, though, suffered from the absence of Frank Robinson, traded to the Dodgers the previous December. The O's were 38-51 in games decided by one or two runs and scored two or fewer runs 66 times. The lack of an attack especially hurt Dave McNally (13-17, 2.95 ERA), who was backed by either one or no runs in 14 games. Jim Palmer (21-10, 2.07), Mike Cuellar (18-12, 2.58) and Pat Dobson (16-18, 2.65) were more fortunate. Boog Powell led the team with 21 home runs and 81 RBIs.

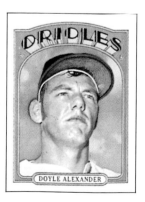

DOYLE ALEXANDER

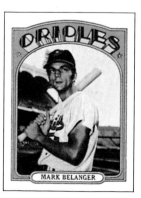

MARK BELANGER

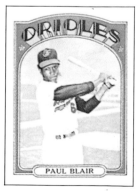

PAUL BLAIR

DON BUFORD

TERRY CROWLEY

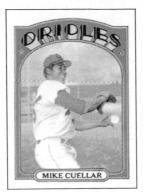

MIKE CUELLAR

PAT DOBSON

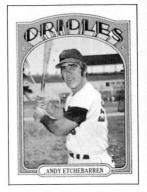

ANDY ETCHEBARREN

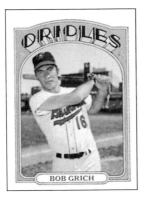

BOB GRICH

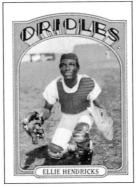

ELLIE HENDRICKS

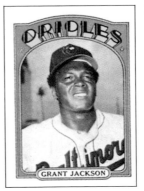

GRANT JACKSON

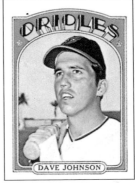

DAVE JOHNSON

DAVE LEONHARD

DAVE McNALLY

DAVE McNALLY

JIM PALMER

BOOG POWELL

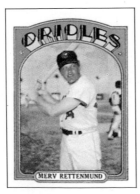

MERV RETTENMUND

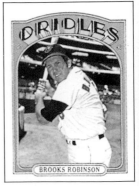

BROOKS ROBINSON

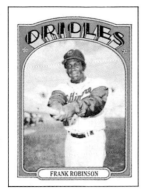

FRANK ROBINSON

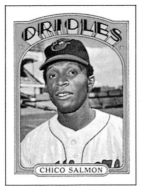

CHICO SALMON

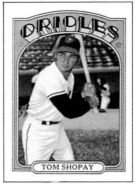

TOM SHOPAY

EDDIE WATT

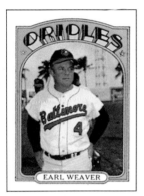

EARL WEAVER

JOHNNY OATES
CATCHER

RORIC HARRISON
PITCHER

DON BAYLOR
OUTFIELD

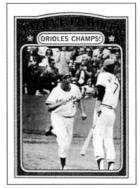

ORIOLES CHAMPS!

GAME No. 1

GAME No. 2

1973

The Orioles blossomed into a daring base-running team and stole a club-record, league-leading 146 bases en route to another American League East title. Their 97-65 record was eight games better than that of runner-up Boston, but Oakland took the league playoffs, 3-2. Earl Weaver began platooning rookie outfielders Al Bumbry and Rich Coggins with Don Baylor and Merv Rettenmund in June and they went on to bat .337 and .319 while stealing 23 and 17 bases, respectively. Bumbry was named Rookie of the Year. Baylor led eight O's who had at least 10 stolen bases each with 32. The team's speed and renewed offensive punch (a club-record .266 batting average) enhanced the Orioles' usual great pitching. Cy Young Award-winner Jim Palmer (22-9, 2.40 ERA) won 20 games for the fourth straight year and led the league in ERA. Mike Cuellar (18-13, 3.27 ERA), Dave McNally (17-17, 3.21) and Doyle Alexander (12-8, 3.86) rounded out the starting staff, while Grant Jackson was 8-0 with a 1.91 ERA and nine saves coming out of the bullpen.

DOYLE
ALEXANDER
BALTIMORE ORIOLES   PITCHER

DON
BAYLOR
BALTIMORE ORIOLES   OUTFIELD

MARK
BELANGER
BALTIMORE ORIOLES   SHORTSTOP

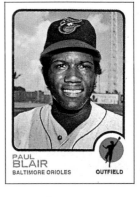

PAUL
BLAIR
BALTIMORE ORIOLES   OUTFIELD

DON
BUFORD
BALTIMORE ORIOLES   OUTFIELD

OUTFIELD

TERRY
CROWLEY
BALTIMORE ORIOLES

MIKE
CUELLAR
BALTIMORE ORIOLES   PITCHER

PAT
DOBSON
BALTIMORE ORIOLES   PITCHER

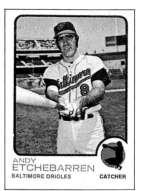

ANDY
ETCHEBARREN
BALTIMORE ORIOLES   CATCHER

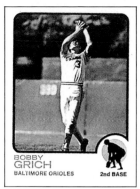

BOBBY
GRICH
BALTIMORE ORIOLES   2nd BASE

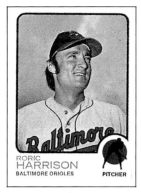

RORIC
HARRISON
BALTIMORE ORIOLES   PITCHER

GRANT
JACKSON
BALTIMORE ORIOLES   PITCHER

TOM
MATCHICK
BALTIMORE ORIOLES   2nd BASE

DAVE
McNALLY
BALTIMORE ORIOLES   PITCHER

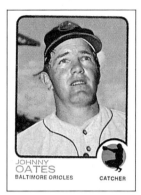

JOHNNY
OATES
BALTIMORE ORIOLES   CATCHER

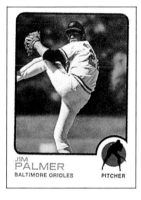

JIM
PALMER
BALTIMORE ORIOLES   PITCHER

**Boyhood Photos
of the Stars**

JIM
PALMER   ★

BOOG
POWELL
BALTIMORE ORIOLES   1st BASE

MERV
RETTENMUND
BALTIMORE ORIOLES   OUTFIELD

BROOKS
ROBINSON
BALTIMORE ORIOLES   3rd BASE

MICKEY
SCOTT
BALTIMORE ORIOLES   PITCHER

EDDIE
WATT
BALTIMORE ORIOLES   PITCHER

COACHES GEORGE BAMBERGER   BILLY HUNTER
JIM FREY   GEORGE STALLER

EARL
WEAVER
BALTIMORE ORIOLES   MANAGER

EARL
WILLIAMS
BALTIMORE ORIOLES   CATCHER

BALTIMORE ORIOLES

1974

Baltimore won its fifth A.L. East championship in six years the hard way. Trailing Boston by eight games with five weeks to go, the O's went 28-6, including 15 one-run wins, the rest of the way to finish 91-71, two games ahead of the Yankees. The Orioles started their stretch run on Aug. 29 with a 10-game winning streak, including a league-record five straight shutouts and 54 consecutive scoreless innings, but they still had to beat New York in a three-game series in mid-September to move in front. Oakland won the playoffs, 3-1. Mike Cuellar (22-10, 3.11 ERA) paced the club in wins, Ross Grimsley, obtained from Cincinnati in the offseason, was 18-13 with a 3.07 ERA, and Dave McNally went 16-10 with a 3.58 ERA. Jim Palmer, slowed by injuries, fell to 7-12. Grant Jackson (6-4, 2.55 ERA, 12 saves) and Bob Reynolds (7-5, 2.74, 7 saves) were the top relievers. Designated hitter Tommy Davis led the team in batting, .289, and RBIs, 84, and second baseman Bobby Grich hit 19 homers, including three against Minnesota on June 18.

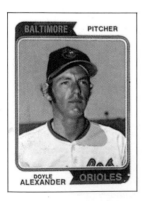

BALTIMORE PITCHER — DOYLE ALEXANDER — ORIOLES

BALTIMORE SHORTSTOP — FRANK BAKER — ORIOLES

BALTIMORE OUTFIELD — DON BAYLOR — ORIOLES

BALTIMORE SHORTSTOP — MARK BELANGER — ORIOLES

BALTIMORE OUTFIELD
PAUL BLAIR
ORIOLES

BALTIMORE OUTFIELD
AL BUMBRY
ORIOLES

BALTIMORE OUTFIELD
RICH COGGINS
ORIOLES

BALTIMORE OUTFIELD
TERRY CROWLEY
ORIOLES

BALTIMORE PITCHER
MIKE CUELLAR
ORIOLES

BALTIMORE DES. HITTER
TOMMY DAVIS
ORIOLES

BALTIMORE CATCHER
ANDY ETCHEBARREN
ORIOLES

BALTIMORE 2nd BASE
BOB GRICH
ORIOLES

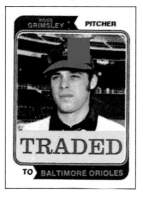

ROSS GRIMSLEY PITCHER
TRADED
TO BALTIMORE ORIOLES

BALTIMORE PITCHER
DON HOOD
ORIOLES

BALTIMORE PITCHER
GRANT JACKSON
ORIOLES

BALTIMORE PITCHER
JESSE JEFFERSON
ORIOLES

BALTIMORE PITCHER
DAVE McNALLY
ORIOLES

BALTIMORE PITCHER
JIM PALMER
ORIOLES

BALTIMORE 1st BASE
BOOG POWELL
ORIOLES

BALTIMORE OUTFIELD
MERV RETTENMUND
ORIOLES

BALTIMORE PITCHER
BOB REYNOLDS ORIOLES

BALTIMORE 3rd BASE
BROOKS ROBINSON ORIOLES

BALTIMORE PITCHER
EDDIE WATT ORIOLES

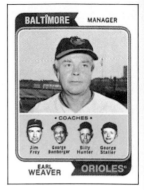

BALTIMORE MANAGER
• COACHES •
Jim Frey George Bamberger Billy Hunter George Staller
EARL WEAVER ORIOLES

BALTIMORE C—1B
EARL WILLIAMS ORIOLES

BALTIMORE ORIOLES

1975

The Orioles compiled the best record in baseball after the All-Star break, 49-25, but they couldn't offset their slow start and ran out of time in their quest for another championship. The O's wound up 90-69, in second place, 4½ games behind Boston. The team was a blend of the familiar and the new. Jim Palmer (23-11, 2.09 ERA) won his second Cy Young Award in three years. He pitched 25 complete games and led the majors in ERA and shutouts with 10. Mike Torrez (20-9, 3.06), who along with Ken Singleton came over from Montreal during the offseason, won 20 games for the first time. Mike Cuellar (14-12, 3.66 ERA) hurled two one-hitters and Ross Grimsley won 10 games. Don Baylor hit a team-best 25 home runs and Lee May, acquired from Houston during the winter, led the club in RBIs with 99. Mark Belanger, Bobby Grich, Brooks Robinson and Paul Blair each won a Gold Glove, the third straight year the Orioles had four defensive leaders.

DOYLE ALEXANDER — Pitcher

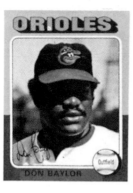

DON BAYLOR — Outfield

MARK BELANGER — Shortstop

PAUL BLAIR — Outfield

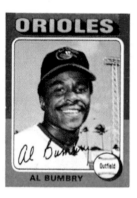

AL BUMBRY — Outfield

ENOS CABELL — 1st Base

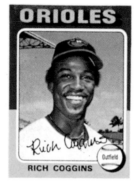

RICH COGGINS — Outfield

MIKE CUELLER — Pitcher

TOMMY DAVIS — Des. Hitter

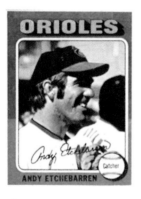

ANDY ETCHEBARREN — Catcher

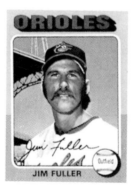

JIM FULLER — Outfield

BOB GRICH — 2nd Base

ROSS GRIMSLEY — Pitcher

ELLIE HENDRICKS — Catcher

DON HOOD — Pitcher

GRANT JACKSON — Pitcher

JESSE JEFFERSON

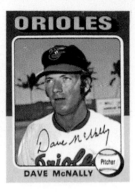

DAVE McNALLY

JIM NORTHRUP

BOB OLIVER

JIM PALMER

BOOG POWELL

BOB. REYNOLDS

BROOKS ROBINSON

EARL WILLIAMS

1976

Two of the biggest trades of the year changed the look of the Orioles. A week before the start of the season, Baltimore sent Don Baylor, Mike Torrez and Paul Mitchell to Oakland for Reggie Jackson and Ken Holtzman. On June 15 the O's traded Holtzman, Doyle Alexander, Grant Jackson, Elrod Hendricks and Jimmy Freeman to the Yankees for pitchers Rudy May, Tippy Martinez, Dave Pagan and Scott McGregor and catcher Rick Dempsey. Jackson didn't report for a month but wound up hitting .277 with 27 homers, 91 RBIs and 28 stolen bases. Rudy May (15-10, 3.72 ERA overall) had the best year of his career, going 11-7 with Baltimore. Martinez (3-1, 2.59 ERA, 8 saves with the O's) was an effective reliever. Jim Palmer (22-13, 2.51 ERA) won his third Cy Young Award in four years, leading the league in wins. Wayne Garland (20-7, 2.68 ERA) began the year in the bullpen but soon joined Palmer as a stellar starter. Lee May led the league with 109 RBIs. The O's finished 88-74, in second place, 10½ games behind the Yankees.

DOYLE ALEXANDER
PITCHER ORIOLES

DON BAYLOR
OUTFIELD ORIOLES

MARK BELANGER
SHORTSTOP ORIOLES

PAUL BLAIR
OUTFIELD ORIOLES

AL BUMBRY
OUTFIELD ORIOLES

MIKE CUELLAR
PITCHER ORIOLES

TOMMY DAVIS
DES. HITTER ORIOLES

DOUG DeCINCES
SECOND BASE ORIOLES

CATCHER DAVE DUNCAN ORIOLES

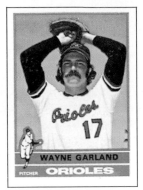

PITCHER WAYNE GARLAND ORIOLES

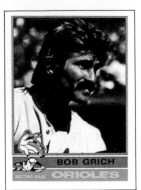

SECOND BASE BOB GRICH ORIOLES

PITCHER ROSS GRIMSLEY ORIOLES

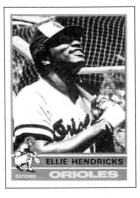

CATCHER ELLIE HENDRICKS ORIOLES

PITCHER GRANT JACKSON ORIOLES

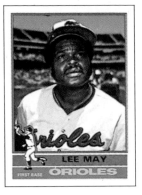

FIRST BASE LEE MAY ORIOLES

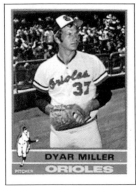

PITCHER DYAR MILLER ORIOLES

PITCHER PAUL MITCHELL ORIOLES

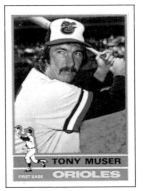

FIRST BASE TONY MUSER ORIOLES

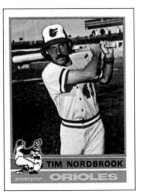

SHORTSTOP TIM NORDBROOK ORIOLES

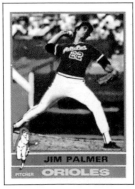

PITCHER JIM PALMER ORIOLES

THIRD BASE BROOKS ROBINSON ORIOLES

OUTFIELD KEN SINGLETON ORIOLES

PITCHER MIKE TORREZ ORIOLES

BALTIMORE ORIOLES

1977

Lightly regarded before the season began because they lost Reggie Jackson, Bobby Grich and Wayne Garland in the first re-entry draft, the Orioles were the surprise team in baseball. They contended all the way and won 20 of their last 27 but couldn't catch the Yankees and ended 97-64, tied for second with the Red Sox, 2½ games behind New York. Designated hitter/first baseman Eddie Murray, the A.L. Rookie of the Year, hit .283 with 27 home runs and 88 RBIs. Ken Singleton (.328, 24 homers, 99 RBIs) was dangerous all year, Lee May drove in 99 runs and Al Bumbry hit .317. Five pitchers, led by Jim Palmer (20-11, 2.91 ERA), won 14 or more games. The others were Rudy May (18-14, 3.61 ERA), Mike Flanagan (15-10, 3.64), Ross Grimsley (14-10, 3.96) and Dennis Martinez (14-7, 4.10). It was the seventh time in eight seasons that Palmer won at least 20. *The Sporting News* named Earl Weaver Manager of the the Year.

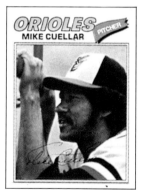

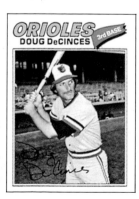
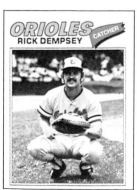

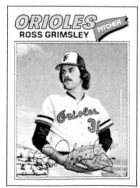

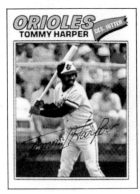

ORIOLES DES. HITTER
TOMMY HARPER

ORIOLES PITCHER
FRED HOLDSWORTH

ORIOLES OUTFIELD
PAT KELLY

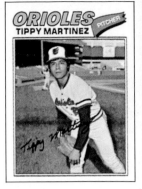

ORIOLES PITCHER
TIPPY MARTINEZ

ORIOLES 1st BASE
LEE MAY

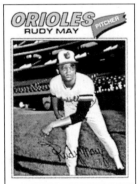

ORIOLES PITCHER
RUDY MAY

ORIOLES PITCHER
DYAR MILLER

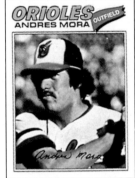

ORIOLES OUTFIELD
ANDRES MORA

ORIOLES 1st BASE
TONY MUSER

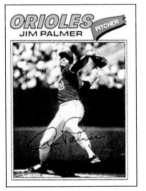

ORIOLES PITCHER
JIM PALMER

ORIOLES 3rd BASE
BROOKS ROBINSON

ORIOLES OUTFIELD
KEN SINGLETON

ORIOLES MANAGER
EARL WEAVER

1978

The Orioles won at least 90 games for the ninth time in 11 years, but that only protected their record as baseball's winningest team over the last 22 seasons. They played and won more one-run games than anyone in the American League, 36-27, but that only helped them to a final 90-71 mark and fourth place, nine games behind the Yankees. Four O's hit at least 20 home runs. Third baseman Doug DeCinces, who concluded the season with a 21-game hitting streak, had 28, Eddie Murray had 25 and a team-high 95 runs driven in, Lee May had 25 and Ken Singleton, who had the best batting average on the club, .293, had 20. All four starting pitchers won at least 15 games: Jim Palmer (21-12, 2.46 ERA), Mike Flanagan (19-15, 4.04), Dennis Martinez (16-11, 3.32) and Scott McGregor (15-13, 3.52). Don Stanhouse saved 24 games and had a 2.88 ERA in 56 appearances. The team led the league in defense for the fifth straight year as second baseman Rich Dauer played 85 consecutive games without an error.

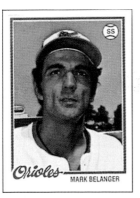
MARK BELANGER

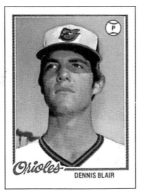
DENNIS BLAIR

NELSON BRILES

AL BUMBRY

RICH DAUER

DOUG DeCINCES

RICK DEMPSEY

MIKE FLANAGAN

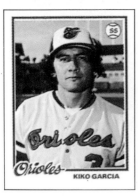

KIKO GARCIA

ROSS GRIMSLEY

LARRY HARLOW

PAT KELLY

DENNY MARTINEZ

TIPPY MARTINEZ

LEE MAY

RUDY MAY

SCOTT McGREGOR

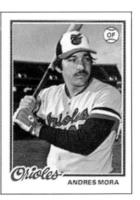

ANDRES MORA

EDDIE MURRAY

TONY MUSER

JIM PALMER

★ ★ ★ ★ ★ ★ ★ ★ ★ ★ ★ ★ ★ ★
MOST CONSECUTIVE SEASONS, ONE CLUB

'77 RECORD
BREAKER ★ ★ ★ ★ ★ ★ ★ BROOKS ROBINSON

KEN SINGLETON

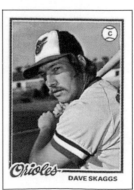

DAVE SKAGGS

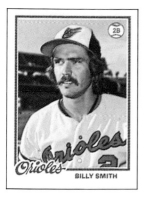

BILLY SMITH

1979

The Orioles regained the American League East crown by eight games over Milwaukee after a five-year shortfall. A 102-57 record, the best in baseball, gave Baltimore its sixth title. The O's then beat California, 3-1, in the playoffs but lost the World Series in seven games to Pittsburgh after leading, 3-1. Consistency and depth were keys. Six pitchers won a minimum of 10 games. Mike Flanagan (23-9, 3.08 ERA) led the majors in wins and was a near unanimous choice as the A.L. Cy Young Award winner. Dennis Martinez (15-16), Scott McGregor (13-6), Steve Stone (11-7), Jim Palmer (10-6) and Tippy Martinez (10-3, 2.88 ERA, 3 saves) were the others. Don Stanhouse (7-3, 2.84 ERA, 21 saves) again was the bullpen ace. Power — a team-record 181 home runs — offset the lack of team speed. Ken Singleton had a career-best 35 homers and 111 RBIs. Eddie Murray drove in 99 runs with 25 homers and Gary Roenicke had 25 home runs. Edward Bennett Williams, a Washington lawyer, purchased the team, effective Nov. 1.

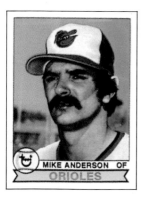

MIKE ANDERSON OF
ORIOLES

MARK BELANGER SS
ORIOLES

NELSON BRILES P
ORIOLES

AL BUMBRY OF
ORIOLES

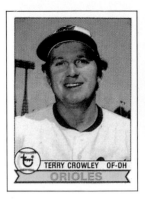

TERRY CROWLEY OF-DH
ORIOLES

RICH DAUER 2B
ORIOLES

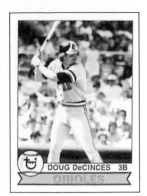

DOUG DeCINCES 3B
ORIOLES

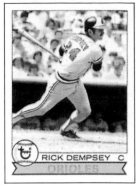

RICK DEMPSEY C
ORIOLES

MIKE FLANAGAN P
ORIOLES

KIKO GARCIA SS
ORIOLES

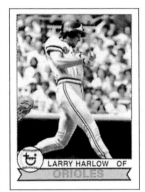

LARRY HARLOW OF
ORIOLES

PAT KELLY OF
ORIOLES

JOE KERRIGAN P
ORIOLES

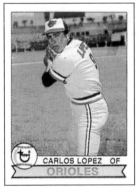

CARLOS LOPEZ OF
ORIOLES

DENNY MARTINEZ P
ORIOLES

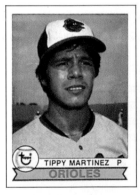

TIPPY MARTINEZ P
ORIOLES

LEE MAY 1B
ORIOLES

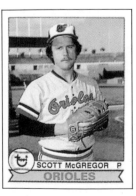

SCOTT McGREGOR P
ORIOLES

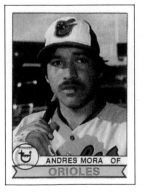

ANDRES MORA OF
ORIOLES

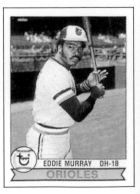

EDDIE MURRAY DH-1B
ORIOLES

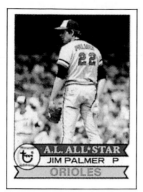

A.L. ALL-STAR
JIM PALMER P
ORIOLES

KEN SINGLETON OF
ORIOLES

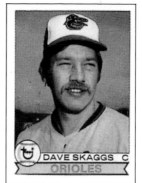

DAVE SKAGGS C
ORIOLES

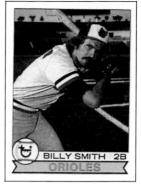

BILLY SMITH 2B
ORIOLES

DON STANHOUSE P
ORIOLES

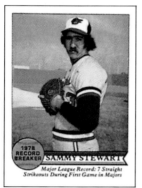

1978 RECORD BREAKER SAMMY STEWART
Major League Record: 7 Straight
Strikeouts During First Game in Majors

ORIOLES 1979 PROSPECTS
SAMMY STEWART PITCHER
JOHN FLINN PITCHER
MARK COREY OUTFIELD

ORIOLES
EARL WEAVER MANAGER

1980

After a slow start owing to injuries, the Orioles became the first team since the 1962 Dodgers to win 100 games (100-62) and not finish first. The O's went 72-32 after June 14 and drew within one-half game of the Yankees on Aug. 28 but never caught them and wound up second, three games out. John Lowenstein and Gary Roenicke, who shared leftfield, and pitchers Scott McGregor and Dennis Martinez missed considerable amounts of time because of injuries. Steve Stone (25-7, 3.23 ERA), who led the majors and set a club-record for wins, gave Baltimore another Cy Young Award winner. McGregor (20-8), Jim Palmer (16-10) and Mike Flanagan (16-13) filled out the starting staff. Tim Stoddard had a team-record 26 saves. Eddie Murray had a career-high 32 home runs and 116 RBIs and batted .300. Ken Singleton rallied to go .304, 24 homers and 104 RBIs. Al Bumbry also was outstanding with a .318 average, 118 runs, a team-record 205 hits and a career-best 44 stolen bases. The team batted .273.

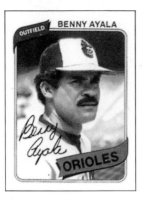

OUTFIELD — BENNY AYALA — ORIOLES

SHORTSTOP — MARK BELANGER — ORIOLES

OUTFIELD — AL BUMBRY — ORIOLES

OF-DH — TERRY CROWLEY — ORIOLES

2nd BASE — RICH DAUER — ORIOLES

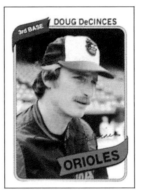

3rd BASE — DOUG DeCINCES — ORIOLES

CATCHER — RICK DEMPSEY — ORIOLES

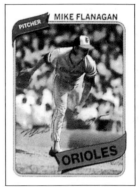

PITCHER — MIKE FLANAGAN — ORIOLES

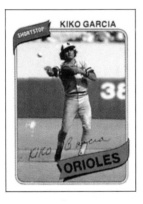

SHORTSTOP — KIKO GARCIA — ORIOLES

OUTFIELD — PAT KELLY — ORIOLES

OUTFIELD — JOHN LOWENSTEIN — ORIOLES

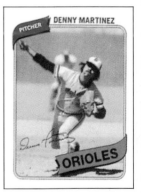

PITCHER — DENNY MARTINEZ — ORIOLES

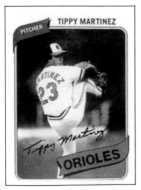

PITCHER — TIPPY MARTINEZ — ORIOLES

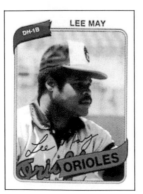

DH-1B — LEE MAY — ORIOLES

PITCHER — SCOTT McGREGOR — ORIOLES

1st BASE — EDDIE MURRAY — ORIOLES

PITCHER · JIM PALMER
ORIOLES

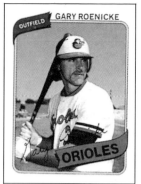

OUTFIELD · GARY ROENICKE
ORIOLES

OUTFIELD · KEN SINGLETON
ORIOLES

CATCHER · DAVE SKAGGS
ORIOLES

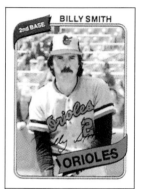

2nd BASE · BILLY SMITH
ORIOLES

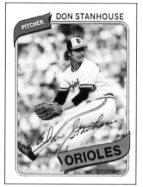

PITCHER · DON STANHOUSE
ORIOLES

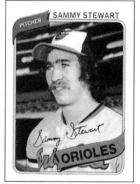

PITCHER · SAMMY STEWART
ORIOLES

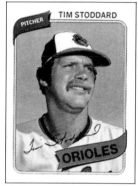

PITCHER · TIM STODDARD
ORIOLES

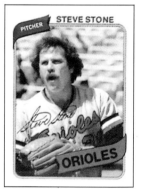

PITCHER · STEVE STONE
ORIOLES

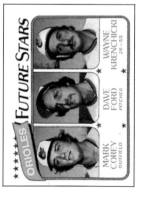

FUTURE STARS
ORIOLES
WAYNE KRENCHICKI 2B — SS
DAVE FORD PITCHER
MARK COREY OUTFIELD

mgr EARL WEAVER
ORIOLES

≡1981

In a strike-interrupted season the Orioles, basically a young team, finished 59-46, in second place, one game behind Milwaukee in the overall American League East standings. Dennis Martinez (14-5, 3.32 ERA), who tied for the league lead in wins and Scott McGregor (13-5, 3.26) were the only consistent starters. Injuries affected Mike Flanagan (9-6, 4.19 ERA), Jim Palmer (7-8, 3.76) and Steve Stone (4-7, 4.57). Tippy Martinez (3-3, 2.90 ERA, 11 saves), Sammy Stewart (4-8, 2.33, 4 saves) and Tim Stoddard (4-2, 3.89, 7 saves) comprised the bullpen. Eddie Murray (.294, 22 home runs, 78 RBIs) had another big year but Ken Singleton fell off to .278, 13, 49. Murray tied for the league high in homers and led the A.L. in RBIs. The team hit five grand slams, including two each by Murray and Doug DeCinces. The Orioles were second in the first half of the season (31-23, two games behind the Yankees) and fourth in the second half (28-23, two games behind Milwaukee) in this abnormal baseball year.

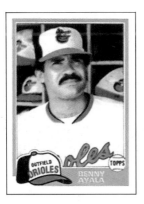
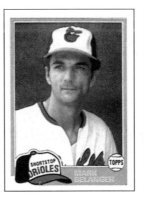

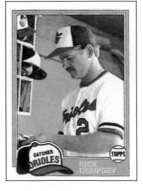

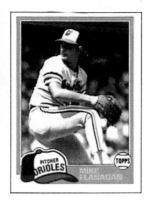

PITCHER ORIOLES
MIKE FLANAGAN
TOPPS

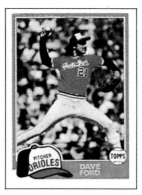

PITCHER ORIOLES
DAVE FORD
TOPPS

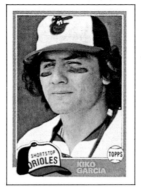

SHORTSTOP ORIOLES
KIKO GARCIA
TOPPS

CATCHER ORIOLES
DAN GRAHAM
TOPPS

OUTFIELD ORIOLES
JOHN LOWENSTEIN
TOPPS

PITCHER ORIOLES
DENNY MARTINEZ
TOPPS

PITCHER ORIOLES
TIPPY MARTINEZ
TOPPS

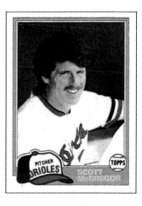

PITCHER ORIOLES
SCOTT McGREGOR
TOPPS

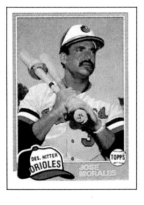

DES. HITTER ORIOLES
JOSE MORALES
TOPPS

1st BASE ORIOLES
EDDIE MURRAY
TOPPS

PITCHER ORIOLES
JIM PALMER
TOPPS

OUTFIELD ORIOLES
GARY ROENICKE
TOPPS

2nd BASE ORIOLES
LENN SAKATA
TOPPS

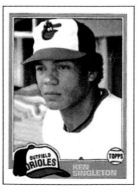

OUTFIELD ORIOLES
KEN SINGLETON
TOPPS

PITCHER ORIOLES
SAMMY STEWART
TOPPS

PITCHER ORIOLES
TIM STODDARD
TOPPS

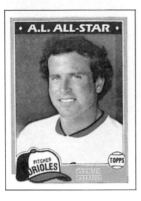
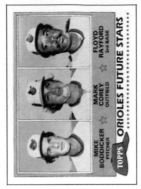

1982

The Orioles almost rewarded Earl Weaver, who announced this would be his last season, with another championship. They tied the Brewers for the lead by beating them in the first three games of a season-ending, four-game series, only to lose the finale, 10-2. To achieve their 94-68 record, the O's had to play the best baseball in the majors, 50-30, including a team-record 27-5 streaks, after the All-Star Game. Eddie Murray (.316, 32 home runs, 110 RBIs) finished in the top seven in the league in seven offensive categories. Rookie of the Year Cal Ripken, Jr., who moved from third to shortstop on July 1, wound up .264, 28 homers, 93 RBIs. John Lowenstein (.320, 24 homers, 66 RBIs) and Gary Roenicke (.270, 21, 74) shared leftfield. Jim Palmer (15-5, 3.13 ERA) won 11 straight and pitched the sixth one-hitter of his career. Dennis Martinez (16-12), Mike Flanagan (15-11), Scott McGregor (14-12) and Sammy Stewart (10-9) also won big while the bullpen relied on Tippy Martinez (8-8, 3.41, 16 saves, a club-record 76 appearances).

ORIOLES
OUTFIELD BENNY AYALA

ORIOLES
SHORTSTOP MARK BELANGER

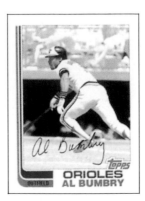

ORIOLES
OUTFIELD AL BUMBRY

ORIOLES
DH 1B TERRY CROWLEY

ORIOLES
2nd BASE · RICH DAUER

ORIOLES
3rd BASE · DOUG DeCINCES

ORIOLES
CATCHER · RICK DEMPSEY

ORIOLES
OF-1B · JIM DWYER

ORIOLES
PITCHER · MIKE FLANAGAN

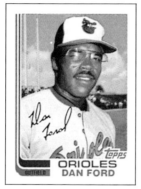

ORIOLES
OUTFIELD · DAN FORD

ORIOLES
PITCHER · DAVE FORD

ORIOLES
CATCHER · DAN GRAHAM

ORIOLES
3B-SS · WAYNE KRENCHICKI

ORIOLES
OUTFIELD · JOHN LOWENSTEIN

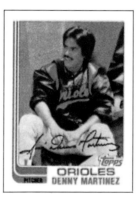

ORIOLES
PITCHER · DENNY MARTINEZ

ORIOLES
PITCHER · TIPPY MARTINEZ

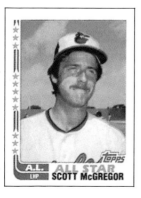

A.L.
LHP · ALL STAR · SCOTT McGREGOR

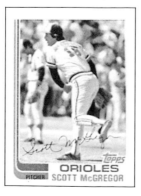

ORIOLES
PITCHER · SCOTT McGREGOR

ORIOLES
DH · JOSE MORALES

ORIOLES
1st BASE · EDDIE MURRAY

ORIOLES
CATCHER JOE NOLAN

ORIOLES
PITCHER JIM PALMER

JIM PALMER
in action

ORIOLES
3rd BASE CAL RIPKEN

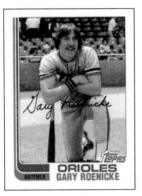

ORIOLES
OUTFIELD GARY ROENICKE

ORIOLES
2nd BASE LENN SAKATA

ORIOLES
OUTFIELD KEN SINGLETON

A.L. ALL STAR
OUTFIELD KEN SINGLETON

ORIOLES
PITCHER SAMMY STEWART

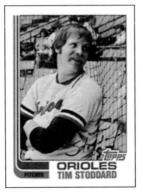

ORIOLES
PITCHER TIM STODDARD

ORIOLES
PITCHER STEVE STONE

BALTIMORE ORIOLES
'81 BATTING & PITCHING LDRS.

BALTIMORE ORIOLES
FUTURE STARS
JEFF SCHNEIDER Pitcher
CAL RIPKEN 3rd Base
BOB BONNER Shortstop

1983

Under new manager Joe Altobelli the Orioles won their seventh divisional title, sixth pennant and third World Championship. They took the East lead for good on Aug. 26, finished 98-64 to beat the Tigers by six games, ousted the White Sox in four games in the League Championship Series and dumped Philadelphia in five games in the World Series. Scott McGregor (18-7, 3.18 ERA) and rookie Mike Boddicker (16-8, 2.77), recalled in mid-May, were a solid one-two pitching combo. Storm Davis (13-7, 3.59 ERA) also was effective as was Mike Flanagan, who was 12-4 with a 3.30 ERA despite missing 10 weeks. Tippy Martinez (9-3, 2.35 ERA) had a career-best 21 saves. A.L. Most Valuable Player Cal Ripken, Jr., (.318, 27 home runs, 102 RBIs) led the league in runs, 121, and hits, 211, while playing every inning at shortstop. Eddie Murray (.306, 33 homers, 111 RBIs) was second in the MVP voting. Ken Singleton rebounded to .276, 18 home runs, 84 RBIs. Altobelli played six outfielders and they all contributed. Attendance broke two million for the first time in Baltimore.

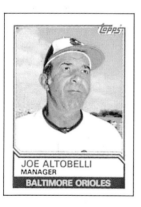

JOE ALTOBELLI
MANAGER
BALTIMORE ORIOLES

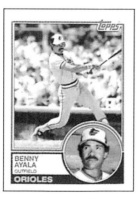

BENNY
AYALA
OUTFIELD
ORIOLES

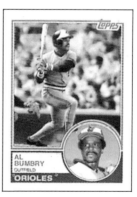

AL
BUMBRY
OUTFIELD
ORIOLES

TERRY
CROWLEY
DH-1st BASE
ORIOLES

RICH
DAUER
2nd BASE
ORIOLES

STORM
DAVIS
PITCHER
ORIOLES

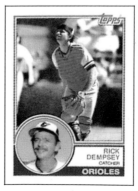

RICK
DEMPSEY
CATCHER
ORIOLES

JIM
DWYER
OUTFIELD-1st BASE
ORIOLES

MIKE
FLANAGAN
PITCHER
ORIOLES

DAN
FORD
OUTFIELD
ORIOLES

GLENN
GULLIVER
3rd BASE
ORIOLES

LEO
HERNANDEZ
3rd BASE
ORIOLES

JOHN
LOWENSTEIN
OUTFIELD
ORIOLES

DENNY
MARTINEZ
PITCHER
ORIOLES

TIPPY
MARTINEZ
PITCHER
ORIOLES

SCOTT
McGREGOR
PITCHER
ORIOLES

EDDIE
MURRAY
1st BASE
ORIOLES

JOE
NOLAN
CATCHER
ORIOLES

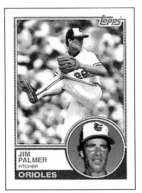

JIM
PALMER
PITCHER
ORIOLES

SUPER VETERAN · JIM PALMER
1983
1965

FLOYD
RAYFORD
3rd BASE
ORIOLES

CAL
RIPKEN
SHORTSTOP
ORIOLES

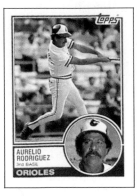

AURELIO
RODRIGUEZ
3rd BASE
ORIOLES

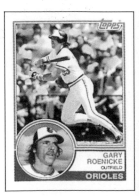

GARY
ROENICKE
OUTFIELD
ORIOLES

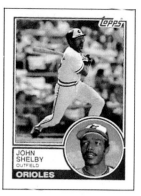

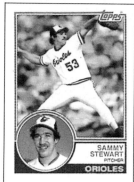

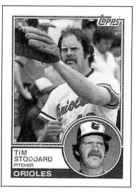

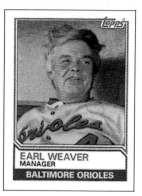

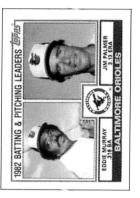

1984

Eddie Murray, Cal Ripken, Jr., and Mike Boddicker kept the Orioles in third place much of the season but the team never put together a hot streak and eventually finished 85-77, in fifth, 19 games in back of the runaway Tigers. Murray, who had a 22-game hitting streak, led the team in batting average, .306, home runs, 29, and RBIs, 110, and led the A.L. in on-base percentage, .410, and game-winning RBIs, 19. Ripken (.304, 27 home runs, 86 RBIs) led the team in runs, 103, and hits, 195. Boddicker (20-11, 2.79 ERA) was the league's only 20-game winner, led the A.L. in ERA and pitched a one-hitter against Toronto on Aug. 13. Storm Davis (14-9, 3.12 ERA) became a starter when Jim Palmer was released in mid-May. McGregor won 15 games despite missing September with a broken finger and Mike Flanagan won 13. Tippy Martinez and Sammy Stewart saved 17 and 13 games, respectively. Injuries took their toll as Dan Ford, Joe Nolan, Jim Dwyer and McGregor all missed extensive time.

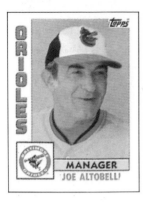
MANAGER
JOE ALTOBELLI

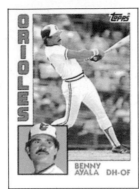
BENNY AYALA DH-OF

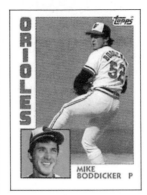
MIKE BODDICKER P

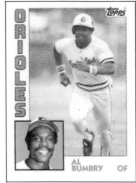
AL BUMBRY OF

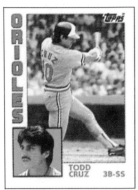
TODD CRUZ 3B-SS

RICH DAUER 2B

STORM DAVIS P

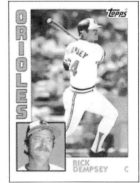
RICK DEMPSEY C

JIM DWYER OF

MIKE FLANAGAN P

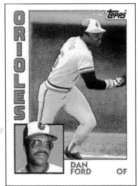
DAN FORD OF

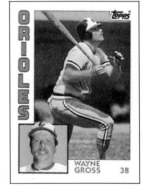
WAYNE GROSS 3B

LEO HERNANDEZ 3B

JOHN LOWENSTEIN OF

DENNY MARTINEZ P

TIPPY MARTINEZ P

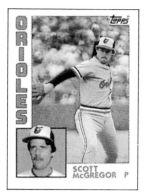

ORIOLES
SCOTT McGREGOR P

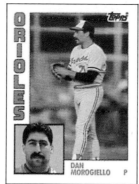

ORIOLES
DAN MOROGIELLO P

ORIOLES
EDDIE MURRAY 1B

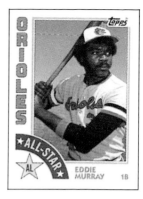

ORIOLES
★ALL-STAR★
AL
EDDIE MURRAY 1B

ORIOLES
JOE NOLAN C

ORIOLES
JIM PALMER P

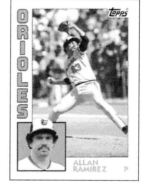

ORIOLES
ALLAN RAMIREZ P

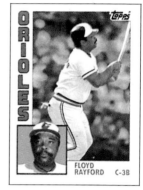

ORIOLES
FLOYD RAYFORD C-3B

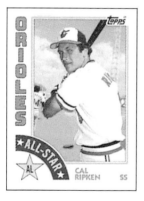

ORIOLES
★ALL-STAR★
AL
CAL RIPKEN SS

ORIOLES
CAL RIPKEN SS

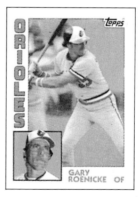

ORIOLES
GARY ROENICKE OF

ORIOLES
LENN SAKATA SS-2B

ORIOLES
JOHN SHELBY OF

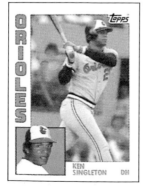

ORIOLES
KEN SINGLETON DH

ORIOLES
SAMMY STEWART P

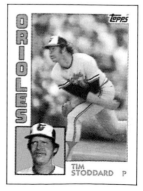

ORIOLES
TIM STODDARD P

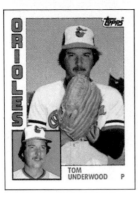

1985

A potent offense produced 818 runs and a major league-leading 214 home runs, both club records, but uncharacteristically average pitching prevented anything better than an 83-78, fourth-place finish, 16 games behind Toronto. Eddie Murray (.297, 31 homers, 124 RBIs, 111 runs) and Cal Ripken, Jr. (.282, 26, 110, 116), again were the offensive cornerstones. Leftfielder Mike Young (.273, 28 homers, 81 RBIs) came on strong in his second full season. Newly signed free agents Fred Lynn (.263, 23 homers, 68 RBIs) and Lee Lacy (.293, 9, 48, 10 stolen bases) did their share when healthy. Reliever Don Aase, another free agent, went 10-6 with 14 saves but starters Scott McGregor (14-14), Dennis Martinez (13-11) and Storm Davis (10-8) all had high ERAs. Mike Boddicker wound up 12-17 after a 6-1 start. Mike Flanagan (4-5, 5.13 ERA), who ruptured an Achilles heel in the winter, could make only 15 starts. Earl Weaver returned as manager in mid-June, replacing Joe Altobelli. Attendance was a franchise-record 2,132,387.

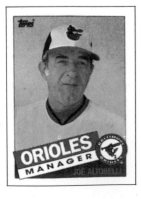

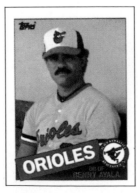

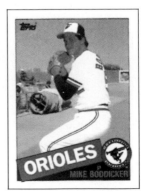

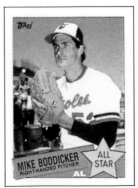

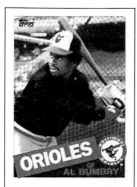

ORIOLES
AL BUMBRY

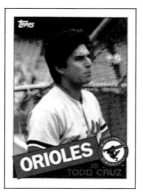

ORIOLES
2B TODD CRUZ

ORIOLES
2B RICH DAUER

ORIOLES
STORM DAVIS

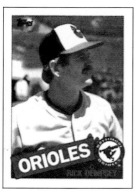

ORIOLES
RICK DEMPSEY

ORIOLES
DH/1B JIM DWYER

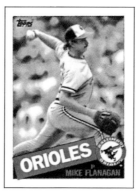

ORIOLES
P MIKE FLANAGAN

ORIOLES
DAN FORD

ORIOLES
OF WAYNE GROSS

ORIOLES
JOHN LOWENSTEIN

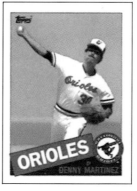

ORIOLES
DENNY MARTINEZ

ORIOLES
TIPPY MARTINEZ

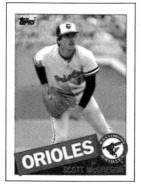

ORIOLES
SCOTT McGREGOR

ORIOLES
EDDIE MURRAY

EDDIE MURRAY
FIRST BASE
AL
ALL STAR

ORIOLES
C JOE NOLAN

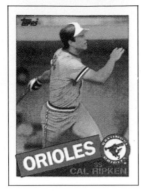
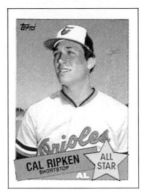

1986

With centerfielder Fred Lynn in the lineup, the Orioles were good. Without him, they weren't. And, partially because injuries limited Lynn to 112 games, the O's finished last for the first time. With Lynn (.287, 23 home runs, 67 RBIs) they were 58-55; without him, 15-34. A season-ending slump of 14-42, beginning on Aug. 6 when the team was 2½ games out of first, led to a final 73−89 record, 22½ games behind Boston. Cal Ripken, Jr. (.282, 25 homers, 81 RBIs), who played every inning for the fourth straight year, and Eddie Murray (.306, 17, 84), who spent time on the disabled list for the first time, were the most reliable offensive performers. Beyond reliever Don Aase, pitching was a major disappointment. Aase had a 2.98 ERA and his 34 saves were a record for a pitcher with a last-place team. Mike Boddicker went 14-12, but he started 14-5. Ken Dixon was 11-13 and Scott McGregor 11-15. Manager Earl Weaver retired for the second time and was replaced immediately after the season by coach Cal Ripken, Sr.

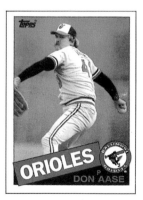
DON AASE

DON AASE

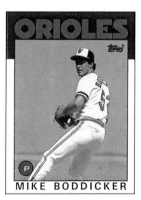
MIKE BODDICKER

RICH DAUER

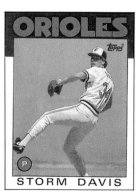
STORM DAVIS

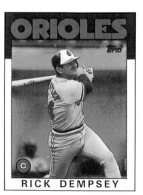
RICK DEMPSEY

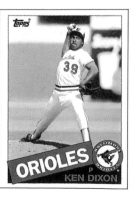
KEN DIXON

KEN DIXON

JIM DWYER

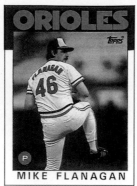

MIKE FLANAGAN

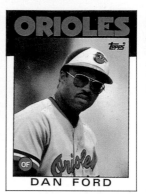

DAN FORD

WAYNE GROSS

LEE LACY

LEE LACY

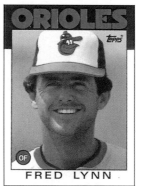

FRED LYNN

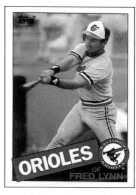

FRED LYNN

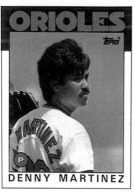

DENNY MARTINEZ

TIPPY MARTINEZ

SCOTT McGREGOR

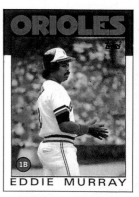

EDDIE MURRAY

JOE NOLAN

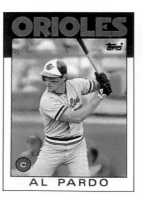

AL PARDO

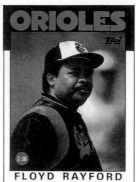

FLOYD RAYFORD

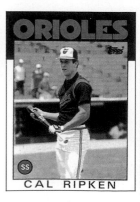

CAL RIPKEN

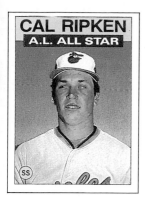

CAL RIPKEN
A.L. ALL STAR

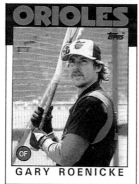

GARY ROENICKE

LENN SAKATA

ORIOLES
DH-OF
LARRY SHEETS

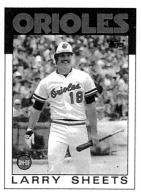

LARRY SHEETS

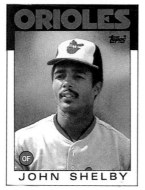

JOHN SHELBY

ORIOLES
NATE SNELL

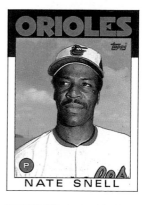

NATE SNELL

SAMMY STEWART

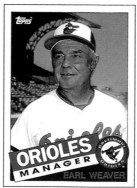

ORIOLES
MANAGER
EARL WEAVER

EARL WEAVER

ALAN WIGGINS

MIKE YOUNG

ORIOLES LEADERS

1987

Cal Ripken's maiden managerial season resulted in the Orioles' second straight sub-par finish in the A.L. East. The Birds landed sixth with a 67-95 record and it was produced by a lack of both offense and pitching.

Despite hitting 211 homers, the Orioles batted .252 as a club and scored 729 runs, the fewest in the American League. The pitchers turned in a composite 5.01 earned run average.

Dave Schmidt (10-5), Mike Boddicker (10-12) and rookie southpaw Eric Bell (10-13) were the top winners on the staff. Except for Schmidt, who had a 3.77 ERA, every other Baltimore pitcher's ERA was above 4.00. Tom Niedenfuer, the former Dodgers' righthander, relieved in 45 games and posted the most saves, 13.

Switchhitting outfielder Larry Sheets paced the regulars at bat with a .316 average. He was tops in homers with 31 and had 94 runs batted in. Veteran Eddie Murray (.277) followed Sheets in the power department with 30 four-baggers and 91 RBIs. Shortstop Cal Ripken Jr., the manager's son, batted .252 and finished with 27 four-baggers and a team-high 98 RBIs.

Fred Lynn batted .253 and contributed 23 homers while driving in 60 runs. Catcher Terry Kennedy, a .250 hitter, had 18 homers and 62 RBIs. Rookie Billy Ripken, the skipper's other son, appeared in 58 games, all at second base, and hit .308. But his homers (two) and RBIs (20) indicated he lacked big brother Cal's power at the plate.

DON AASE

ERIC BELL

JUAN BENIQUEZ

MIKE BODDICKER

JUAN BONILLA

RICH BORDI

STORM DAVIS

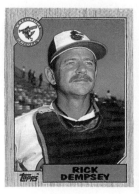
RICK DEMPSEY

KEN
DIXON

JIM
DWYER

MIKE
FLANAGAN

KEN
GERHART

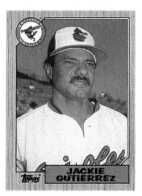

JACKIE
GUTIERREZ

BRAD
HAVENS

TERRY
KENNEDY

RAY
KNIGHT

LEE
LACY

FRED
LYNN

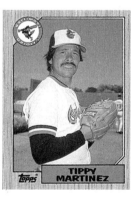

TIPPY
MARTINEZ

SCOTT
McGREGOR

EDDIE
MURRAY

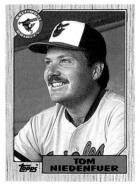

TOM
NIEDENFUER

TOM
O'MALLEY

FLOYD
RAYFORD

CAL RIPKEN

CAL RIPKEN
ALL STAR

CAL RIPKEN, SR.

DAVE SCHMIDT

LARRY SHEETS

JOHN SHELBY

NATE SNELL

JOHN STEFERO

JIM TRABER

EARL WEAVER

ALAN WIGGINS

MIKE YOUNG

ORIOLES LEADERS

1988

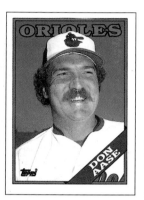

DON AASE

JEFF BALLARD

ERIC BELL

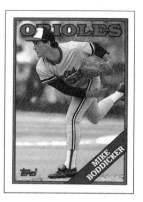

MIKE BODDICKER

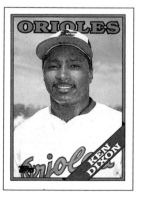

KEN DIXON

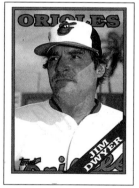

JIM DWYER

KEN GERHART

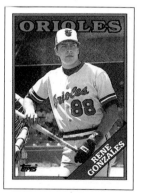

RENE GONZALES

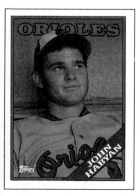

JOHN HABYAN

MIKE HART

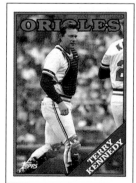

TERRY KENNEDY

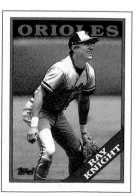

RAY KNIGHT

LEE LACY

FRED LYNN

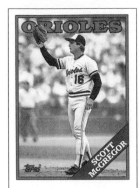

SCOTT McGREGOR

'87 RECORD BREAKERS

EDDIE MURRAY

TOM NIEDENFUER

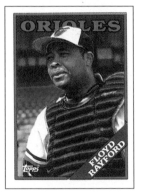

FLOYD RAYFORD

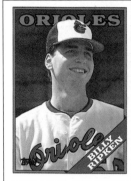

BILLY RIPKEN

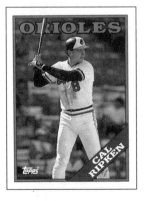

CAL RIPKEN

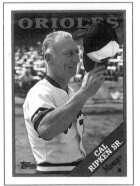

CAL RIPKEN SR.

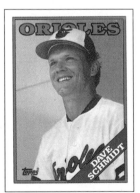

DAVE SCHMIDT

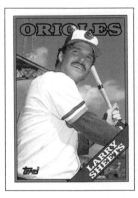

LARRY SHEETS

JIM TRABER

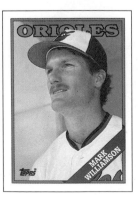

MARK WILLIAMSON

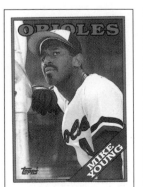

MIKE YOUNG

ORIOLES Leaders

COLLECTORS' CORNER

1951: Blue Back of Johnny Mize (50) lists for $25 . . . Red Back of Duke Snider (38) lists for $18 . . . Complete set of 9 Team Cards lists for $900 . . . Complete set of 11 Connie Mack All-Stars lists for $2750 with Babe Ruth and Lou Gehrig listing for $700 each . . . Current All-Stars of Jim Konstanty, Robin Roberts and Eddie Stanky list for $4000 each . . . Complete set lists for $14,250.

1952: Mickey Mantle (311) is unquestionably the most sought-after post-war gum card, reportedly valued at $6,500-plus . . . Ben Chapman (391) is photo of Sam Chapman . . . Complete set lists in excess of $36,000.

1953: Mickey Mantle (82) and Willie Mays (244) list for $1,500 each . . . Set features first TOPPS card of Hall-of-Famer Whitey Ford (207) and only TOPPS card of Hall-of-Famer Satchel Paige (220). Pete Runnels (219) is photo of Don Johnson . . . Complete set lists for $9,500.

1954: Ted Williams is depicted on two cards (1 and 250) . . . Set features rookie cards of Hank Aaron (128), Ernie Banks (94) and Al Kaline (201) . . . Card of Aaron lists for $650 . . . Card of Willie Mays (90) lists for $200 . . . Complete set lists for $5,500.

1955: Set features rookie cards of Sandy Koufax (123), Harmon Killebrew (124) and Roberto Clemente (164) . . . The Clemente and Willie Mays (194) cards list for $425 each . . .Complete set lists for $3,900.

1956: Set features rookie cards of Hall-of-Famers Will Harridge (1), Warren Giles (2), Walter Alston (8) and Luis Aparicio (292) . . . Card of Mickey Mantle (135) lists for $650 . . . Card of Willie Mays (130) lists for $125 . . . Complete set lists for $4,000 . . . The Team Cards are found both dated (1955) and undated and are valued at $15 (dated) and more . . . There are two unnumbered Checklist Cards valued high.

1957: Set features rookie cards of Don Drysdale (18), Frank Robinson (35) and Brooks Robinson (328) . . . A reversal of photo negative made Hank Aaron (20) appear as a left-handed batter . . . Card of Mickey Mantle (95) lists for $600 . . . Cards of Brooks Robinson and Sandy Koufax (302) list for $275 each . . . Complete set lists for $4,800.

1958: Set features first TOPPS cards of Casey Stengel (475) and Stan Musial (476) . . . Mike McCormick (37) is photo of Ray Monzant . . . Milt Bolling (188) is photo of Lou Berberet . . . Bob Smith (226) is photo of Bobby Gene Smith . . . Card of Mickey Mantle (150) lists for $400 . . . Card of Ted Williams (1) lists for $325 . . . Complete set lists for $4,800.

1959: In a notable error, Lou Burdette (440) is shown posing as a left-handed pitcher . . . Set features rookie card of Bob Gibson (514) . . . Ralph Lumenti (316) is photo of Camilo Pascual . . . Card of Gibson lists for $200 . . . Card of Mickey Mantle (10) lists for $300 . . . Complete set lists for $3,000.

1960: A run of 32 consecutively numbered rookie cards (117-148) includes the first card of Carl Yastrzemski (148) . . . J.C. Martin (346) is photo of Gary Peters . . . Gary Peters (407) is photo of J.C. Martin . . . Card of Yastrzemski lists for $150 . . . Card of Mickey Mantle (350) lists for $300 . . . Complete set lists for $2,600.

1961: The Warren Spahn All-Star (589) should have been numbered 587 . . . Set features rookie cards of Billy Williams (141) and Juan Marichal (417) . . . Dutch Dotterer (332) is photo of his brother, Tommy . . . Card of Mickey Mantle (300) lists for $200 . . . Card of Carl Yastrzemski (287) lists for $90 . . . Complete set lists for $3,600.

1962: Set includes special Babe Ruth feature (135-144) . . . some Hal Reniff cards numbered 139 should be 159 . . . Set features rookie card of Lou Brock (387) . . . Gene Freese (205) is shown posing as a left-handed batter . . . Card of Mickey Mantle (200) lists for $325 . . . Card of Carl Yastrzemski (425) lists for $125 . . . Complete set lists for $3,300.

1963: Set features rookie card of Pete Rose (537), which lists for $500-plus . . . Bob Uecker (126) is shown posing as a left-handed batter . . . Don Landrum (113) is photo of Ron Santo . . . Eli Grba (231) is photo of Ryne Duren . . . Card of Mickey Mantle (200) lists for $200 . . . Card of Lou Brock (472) lists for $75 . . . Complete set lists for $2,900.

1964: Set features rookie cards of Richie Allen (243), Tony Conigliaro (287) and Phil Niekro (541) . . . Lou Burdette is again shown posing as a left-handed pitcher . . . Bud Bloomfield (532) is photo of Jay Ward . . . Card of Pete Rose (125) lists for $150 . . . Card of Mickey Mantle (50) lists for $175 . . . Complete set lists for $1,600.

1965: Set features rookie cards of Dave Johnson (473), Steve Carlton (477) and Jim Hunter (526) . . . Lew Krausse (462) is photo of Pete Lovrich . . . Gene Freese (492) is again shown posing as a left-handed batter . . . Cards of Carlton and Pete Rose (207) list for $135 . . . Card of Mickey Mantle (350) lists for $300 . . . Complete set lists for $800.

1966: Set features rookie card of Jim Palmer (126) . . . For the third time (see 1962 and 1965) Gene Freese (319) is shown posing as a left-handed batter . . . Dick Ellsworth (447) is photo of Ken Hubbs (died February 13, 1964) . . . Card of Gaylord Perry (598) lists for $175 . . . Card of Willie McCovey (550) lists for $80 . . . Complete set lists for $2,500.

1967: Set features rookie cards of Rod Carew (569) and Tom Seaver (581) . . . Jim Fregosi (385) is shown posing as a left-handed batter . . . George Korince (72) is photo of James Brown but was later corrected on a second Korince card (526) . . . Card of Carew lists for $150 . . . Card of Maury Wills (570) lists for $65 . . . Complete set lists for $2,500.

1968: Set features rookie cards of Nolan Ryan (177) and Johnny Bench (247) . . . The special feature of The Sporting News All-Stars (361-380) includes eight players in the Hall of Fame . . . Card of Ryan lists for $135 . . . Card of Bench lists for $125 . . . Complete set lists for $1,200.

1969: Set features rookie card of Reggie Jackson (260) . . . There are two poses each for Clay Dalrymple (151) and Donn Clendenon (208) . . . Aurelio Rodriguez (653) is photo of Lenny Garcia (Angels' bat boy) . . . Card of Mickey Mantle (500) lists for $150 . . . Card of Jackson lists for $175 . . . Complete set lists for $1,200.

1970: Set features rookie cards of Vida Blue (21), Thurman Munson (189) and Bill Buckner (286) . . . Also included are two deceased players Miguel Fuentes (88) and Paul Edmondson (414) who died after cards went to press . . . Card of Johnny Bench (660) lists for $75 . . . Card of Pete Rose (580) lists for $75 . . . Complete set lists for $1,000.

1971: Set features rookie card of Steve Garvey (341) . . . the final series (644-752) is found in lesser quantity and includes rookie card (664) of three pitchers named Reynolds (Archie, Bob and Ken) . . . Card of Garvey lists for $65 . . . Card of Pete Rose (100) lists for $45 . . . Complete set lists for $1,000.

1972: There were 16 cards featuring photos of players in their boyhood years . . . Dave Roberts (91) is photo of Danny Coombs . . . Brewers Rookie Card (162) includes photos of Darrell Porter and Jerry Bell, which were reversed . . . Cards of Steve Garvey (686) and Rod Carew (695) list for $60 . . . Card of Pete Rose (559) lists for $50 . . . Complete set lists for $1,000.

1973: A special Home Run Card (1) depicted Babe Ruth, Hank Aaron and Willie Mays . . . Set features rookie card of Mike Schmidt (615) listing for $175 . . . Joe Rudi (360) is photo of Gene Tenace . . . Card of Pete Rose (130) lists for $18 . . . Card of Reggie Jackson (255) lists for $12.50 . . . Complete set lists for $600.

1974: Set features 15 San Diego Padres cards printed as ''Washington, N.L.'' due to report of franchise move, later corrected . . . Also included was a 44-card Traded Series which updated team changes . . . Set features rookie card of Dave Winfield (456) . . . Card of Mike Schmidt (283) lists for $35 . . . Card of Winfield lists for $25 . . . Complete set lists for $325.

1975: Herb Washington (407) is the only card ever published with position ''designated runner,'' featuring only base-running statistics . . . Set features rookie cards of Robin Yount (223), George Brett (228), Jim Rice (616), Gary Carter (620) and Keith Hernandez (623) . . . Don Wilson (455) died after cards went to press (January 5, 1975) . . . Card of Brett lists for $50 . . . Cards of Rice and Carter list for $35 . . . Complete set lists for $475 . . . TOPPS also tested the complete 660-card series in a smaller size (2¼" x 3 1/8") in certain areas of USA in a limited supply . . . Complete set of ''Mini-Cards'' lists for $700.

1976: As in 1974 there was a 44-card Traded Series . . . Set features five Father & Son cards (66-70) and ten All-Time All-Stars (341-350) . . . Card of Pete Rose (240) lists for $15 . . . Cards of Jim Rice (340), Gary Carter (441) and George Brett (19) list for $12 . . . Complete set lists for $225.

1977: Set features rookie cards of Andre Dawson (473) and Dale Murphy (476) . . . Reuschel Brother Combination (634) shows the two (Paul and Rick) misidentified . . . Dave Collins (431) is photo of Bob Jones . . . Card of Murphy lists for $65 . . . Card of Pete Rose (450) lists for $8.50 . . . Complete set lists for $250.

1978: Record Breakers (1-7) feature Lou Brock, Sparky Lyle, Willie McCovey, Brooks Robinson, Pete Rose, Nolan Ryan and Reggie Jackson . . . Set features rookie cards of Jack Morris (703), Lou Whitaker (704), Paul Molitor/Alan Trammell (707), Lance Parrish (708) and Eddie Murray (36) . . . Card of Murray lists for $35 . . . Card of Parrish lists for $35 . . . Complete set lists for $200.

1979: Bump Wills (369) was originally shown with Blue Jays affiliation but later corrected to Rangers . . . Set features rookie cards of Ozzie Smith (116), Pedro Guerrero (719), Lonnie Smith (722) and Terry Kennedy (724) . . . Larry Cox (489) is photo of Dave Rader . . . Card of Dale Murphy (39) lists for $8 . . . Cards of Ozzie Smith and Eddie Murray (640) list for $7.50 . . . Complete set lists for $135.

1980: Highlights (1-6) feature Hall-of-Famers Lou Brock, Carl Yastrzemski, Willie McCovey and Pete Rose . . . Set features rookie cards of Dave Stieb (77), Rickey Henderson (482) and Dan Quisenberry (667) . . . Card of Henderson lists for $28 . . . Card of Dale Murphy (274) lists for $5.50 . . . Complete set lists for $135.

1981: Set features rookie cards of Fernando Valenzuela (302), Kirk Gibson (315), Harold Baines (347) and Tim Raines (479) . . . Jeff Cox (133) is photo of Steve McCatty . . . John Littlefield (489) is photo of Mark Riggins . . . Card of Valenzuela lists for $7.50 . . . Card of Raines lists for $9 . . . Complete set lists for $80.

1982: Pascual Perez (383) printed with no position on front lists for $35, later corrected . . . Set features rookie cards of Cal Ripken (21), Jesse Barfield (203), Steve Sax (681) and Kent Hrbek (766) . . . Dave Rucker (261) is photo of Roger Weaver . . . Steve Bedrosian (502) is photo of Larry Owen . . . Card of Ripken lists for $12.50 . . . Cards of Barfield and Sax list for $5 . . . Complete set lists for $75.

1983: Record Breakers (1-6) feature Tony Armas, Rickey Henderson, Greg Minton, Lance Parrish, Manny Trillo and John Wathan . . . A series of Super Veterans features early and current photos of 34 leading players . . . Set features rookie cards of Tony Gwynn (482) and Wade Boggs (498) . . . Card of Boggs lists for $32 . . . Card of Gwynn lists for $16 . . . Complete set lists for $85.

1984: Highlights (1-6) salute eleven different players . . . A parade of superstars is included in Active Leaders (701-718) . . . Set features rookie card of Don Mattingly (8) listing for $35 . . . Card of Darryl Strawberry (182) lists for $10 . . . Complete set lists for $85.

1985: A Father & Son Feature (131-143) is again included . . . Set features rookie cards of Scott Bankhead (393), Mike Dunne (395), Shane Mack (398), John Marzano (399), Oddibe McDowell (400), Mark McGwire (401), Pat Pacillo (402), Cory Snyder (403) and Billy Swift (404) as part of salute to 1984 USA Baseball Team (389-404) that participated in Olympic Games plus rookie cards of Roger Clemens (181) and Eric Davis (627) . . . Card of McGwire lists for $20 . . . Card of Davis lists for $18 . . . Card of Clemens lists for $11 . . . Complete set lists for $95.

1986: Set includes Pete Rose Feature (2-7), which reproduces each of Rose's TOPPS cards from 1963 thru 1985 (four per card) . . . Bob Rodgers (141) should have been numbered 171 . . . Ryne Sandberg (690) is the only card with TOPPS logo omitted . . . Complete set lists for $24.

1987: Record Breakers (1-7) feature Roger Clemens, Jim Deshaies, Dwight Evans, Davey Lopes, Dave Righetti, Ruben Sierra and Todd Worrell . . . Jim Gantner (108) is shown with Brewers logo reversed . . . Complete set lists for $22.

1988: Record Breakers (1-7) include Vince Coleman, Don Mattingly, Mark McGwire, Eddie Murray, Phil & Joe Niekro, Nolan Ryan and Benny Santiago. Al Leiter (18) was originally shown with photo of minor leaguer Steve George and later corrected. Complete set lists for $20.00.

PLAYER	G	IP	W	L	R	ER	SO	BB	GS	CG	SHO	SV	ERA
AASE, DON	325	956.2	61	54	428	398	552	371	91	22	5	75	3.74
ADAMSON, MIKE	11	26	0	4			14	22	5	0	0	3	7.27
ALEXANDER, DOYLE	467	2708.1	160	135	1228	1117	1199	803	370	82	13	3	3.71
ANDERSON, JOHN	24	45	0	0			19	14	1	0	0	1	6.40
BAMBERGER, GEORGE	10	14	0	0			3	10	1	0	0	0	9.64
BARBER, STEVE	466	1998	121	106			1309	950	272	59	21	1	3.36
BARNOWSKI, ED	6	7	0	0			8	8	0	0	0	0	2.57
BEAMON, CHARLIE, SR.	27	72	3	3			45	36	5	1	1	0	3.88
BEARDEN, GENE	193	789	45	38			259	435	84	29	7	1	3.96
BEENE, FRED	112	289	12	7			156	111	6	0	0	4	3.61
BENTON, AL	450	1689	98	88			697	733	167	58	10	66	3.66
BERTAINA, FRANK	99	412	19	29			280	214	76	6	5	0	3.84
BICKFORD, VERN	182	1077	66	57			540	467	149	73	9	4	3.71
BIRRER, BABE	56	119	4	3			45	37	3	1	0	1	4.39
BLYZKA, MIKE	70	180	3	11			58	107	9	2	0	1	5.60
BODDICKER, MIKE	136	900.2	63	49	409	360	584	315	126	42	11	0	3.60
BORDI, RICH	155	330.2	17	18	162	147	218	104	11	0	0	10	4.00
BOSWELL, DAVE	205	1065	68	56			882	481	151	37	6	0	3.52
BRABENDER, GENE	151	621	35	43			440	282	80	15	4	6	4.25
BRECHEEN, HARRY	318	1905	133	92			901	536	240	125	25	18	2.92
BRILES, NELSON	452	2112	129	112			1163	547	279	64	17	22	3.43
BROWN, HAL	358	1680	85	92			710	389	211	47	13	11	3.81
BROWN, MARK	15	38.2	1	2			15	14	0	0	0	0	5.12
BRUNET, GEORGE	324	1431	69	93			921	581	213	39	15	4	3.62
BUNKER, WALLY	206	1086	60	52			569	334	152	34	5	3	3.51
BURNSIDE, PETE	196	569	19	36			203	230	64	14	3	7	4.79
BURWELL, BILL	70	218	9	8			49	79	6	1	0	6	4.38
BUZHARDT, JOHN	326	1489	71	96			678	457	200	44	15	6	3.67
BYRD, HARRY	187	827	46	54			381	355	108	33	8	9	4.35
BYRNE, TOMMY	281	1363	85	69			766	1037	170	65	12	12	4.11
CAIN, BOB	140	629	37	44			249	316	89	27	3	0	4.49
CECCARELLI, ART	79	307	9	18			166	147	42	8	3	0	5.04
CHAKALES, BOB	171	420	15	25			187	225	23	3	1	10	4.54
COLEMAN, JOE P.	223	1133	52	76			444	566	140	60	11	6	4.38
COLEMAN, RIP	95	247	7	25			130	124	33	3	1	5	4.59
CONSUEGRA, SANDY	248	810	51	32			193	246	71	24	5	26	3.37
CORBETT, DOUG	302	530	24	28			327	187	1	0	0	65	3.12
CUELLAR, MIKE	453	2807	185	130	206	184	1632	822	379	172	36	11	3.14
DALKOWSKI, STEVE						No major league statistics							
DAVIS, STORM	154	855	54	40	378	347	486	282	121	27	4	1	3.65
DELEON, LUIS	195	309.1	17	17			233	68	0	0	0	31	3.03
DELOCK, IKE	329	1237	84	75			672	530	147	32	6	31	4.04
DILLMAN, BILL	50	155	7	12			86	51	15	2	1	3	4.53
DIXON, KEN	71	377.1	19	18	185	175	286	151	53	5	1	1	4.17
DOBSON, PAT	414	2119	122	129			1301	665	279	74	14	19	3.54
DORISH, HARRY	323	835	45	43			332	301	40	13	4	44	3.83
DRABOWSKY, MOE	589	1640	88	105			1162	702	154	30	6	55	3.71
DRAGO, DICK	519	1876	108	117			987	558	189	62	10	58	3.62
DREWS, KARL	218	827	44	53			322	332	107	26	7	7	4.76
DUKES, TOM	161	217	5	16			169	82	0	0	0	7	4.35
DUREN, RYNE	311	589	27	44			630	392	32	2	1	57	3.83
ESTRADA, CHUCK	412	764	50	44			535	416	105	24	2	6	4.08
FANNIN, CLIFF	164	733	34	51			352	393	98	28	6	6	4.85
FARMER, ED	370	624	30	43			395	345	21	0	0	75	4.30
FARRARESE, DON	183	507	17	36			350	295	50	12	2	5	3.99

PLAYER	G	IP	W	L	R	ER	SO	BB	GS	CG	SHO	SV	ERA
FISHER, EDDIE	690	1541	85	70			812	438	63	7	2	81	3.40
FISHER, JACK	400	1977	86	139			1017	605	265	62	9	9	4.06
FLANAGAN, MIKE	328	2090	136	103	966	892	1175	656	311	94	17	1	3.84
FLINN, JOHN	42	69.2	5	2			36	37	2	1	0	1	4.14
FORD, DAVE	51	155	5	6			46	32	8	0	0	3	4.01
FORNIELES, MIEK	432	1156	63	64			576	421	76	20	4	55	3.96
FOX, HOWIE	248	1108	43	72			342	435	132	42	5	6	4.33
GARLAND, WAYNE	190	1040	55	66			450	328	121	43	7	6	3.89
GARVER, NED	402	2477	129	157			881	881	330	153	18	12	3.73
GRAY, TED	222	1133	59	74			687	595	162	50	7	4	4.37
GRIFFIN, MIKE	41	124.1	4	10			58	37	18	0	0	2	4.49
GRIMSLEY, ROSS	345	2039	124	99			750	559	295	79	15	3	3.81
HADDIX, HARVEY	453	2235	136	113			1575	601	285	99	20	21	3.63
HALL, DICK	495	1259	93	75			741	236	74	20	3	68	3.32
HARDIN, JIM	164	752	43	32			408	202	100	28	7	4	3.18
HARRIS, LUM	151	819	35	63			232	265	91	46	4	1	4.16
HARRISON, RORIC	140	590	30	35			319	257	70	12	0	10	4.24
HARRIST, EARL	132	383	12	28			162	193	24	2	0	10	4.34
HARSHMAN, JACK	217	1168	69	65			741	539	155	61	12	7	3.51
HARTZELL, PAUL	170	703.1	27	39			237	181	87	22	2	12	3.90
HAVENS, BRAD	109	438	21	31	240		267	171	58	6	2	1	4.93
HEARD, JEHOSIE	2	3	0	0			2	3	0	0	0	0	15.00
HETKI, JOHN	214	525	18	26			175	185	23	8	0	13	4.39
HOEFT, BILLY	505	1848	97	101			1140	685	200	75	17	33	3.94
HOGUE, BOBBY	172	327	18	16			108	142	3	0	0	17	3.96
HOLCOMBE, KEN	99	374	18	32			118	170	48	18	2	2	3.99
HOLDSWORTH, FRED	72	183	7	10			94	86	15	0	0	2	4.38
HOLTZMAN, KEN	451	2868	174	150			1601	910	410	127	31	3	3.49
HOOD, DON	297	847.1	34	35			374	364	72	6	1	7	3.79
HOUTTEMAN, ART	325	1556	87	91			639	516	181	78	14	20	4.14
HOWARD, BRUCE	120	529	26	31			349	239	75	7	2	1	3.18
HUFFMAN, PHIL	31	173	6	18			56	68	31	2	0	0	5.77
HYDE, DICK	169	298	17	14			144	137	2	0	0	23	3.56
JACKSON, GRANT	692	1359	86	75			889	511	83	16	5	79	3.46
JEFFERSON, JESSE	237	1086	39	81			522	520	144	25	4	1	4.81
JOHNSON, CONNIE	123	716	40	39			497	257	100	34	8	1	3.44
JOHNSON, DAVE C.	53	109	4	10			50	34	7	0	0	4	4.62
JOHNSON, DON	198	631	27	38			262	285	70	17	4	12	4.78
JOHNSON, ERNIE	273	574	40	23			319	231	19	3	1	19	3.78
JONES, GORDON	171	379	15	18			232	120	21	4	0	12	4.16
JONES, ODELL	152	419.1	17	33			258	161	43	4	0	12	4.51
JONES, SAM	322	1644	102	101			1376	822	222	76	17	9	3.59
KENNEDY, BILL	172	465	15	28			256	289	45	6	0	11	4.70
KERRIGAN, JOE	131	220	8	12			106	92	2	0	0	15	3.89
KINDER, ELLIS	484	1480	102	71			749	539	122	56	10	102	3.43
KNOWLES, DAROLD	765	1091	66	74			681	480	8	1	0	143	3.12
KOSLO, DAVE	348	1592	92	107			606	538	189	74	16	22	3.68
KRETLOW, LOU	199	786	27	47			450	522	104	22	3	1	4.87
KUCAB, JOHN	152	59	5	5			48	51	3	2	0	6	4.44
KUZAVA, BOB	213	862	49	44			446	415	99	34	6	13	4.05
LANIER, MAX	327	1619	108	82			821	611	204	91	21	17	3.01
LARSEN, DON	412	1549	81	91			849	725	171	44	11	23	3.78
LEHMAN, KEN	134	264	14	10			134	95	13	2	0	7	3.92
LEONHARD, DAVE	117	336	16	14			146	150	29	7	2	5	3.16
LITTLEFIELD, DICK	243	761	33	54			495	413	83	16	2	9	4.72

PLAYER	G	IP	W	L	R	ER	SO	BB	GS	CG	SHO	SV	ERA
LOPAT, EDDIE	340	2439	166	112			859	650	318	164	27	3	3.21
LOPEZ, MARCELINO	171	653	31	40			426	317	93	40	3	2	3.62
LUEBBER, STEVE	66	206	6	10			93	106	24	2	1	3	4.63
MABE, BOB	51	143	7	11			82	61	14	4	0	0	4.78
MAHONEY, BOB	36	91	2	5			34	50	4	0	0	0	4.95
MARSHALL, CLARENCE	73	185	7	7			69	158	15	1	0	0	5.98
MARTIN, MORRIE	250	604	38	34			245	251	42	8	1	15	4.29
MARTINEZ, DENNY	338	1873.1	111	99	951	870	921	611	258	70	11	5	4.18
MARTINEZ, TIPPY	543	831	55	42	348	312	629	420	2	0	0	115	3.38
MAY, RUDY	535	2621.1	152	156			1760	958	360	87	24	12	3.46
McCORMICK, MIKE	484	2381	134	128			1321	795	333	91	33	5	3.73
McGREGOR, SCOTT	326	2038.2	136	98	944	869	855	476	290	82	22	5	3.84
McNALLY, DAVE	424	2730	184	119			1512	826	396	120	33	2	3.24
MILLER, BILL	41	132	6	9			72	79	18	5	2	1	4.23
MILLER, DYAR	251	466	23	17			235	177	1	0	0	48	3.23
MILLER, JOHN E.	46	227	12	14			178	138	35	0	0	0	3.89
MILLER, RANDY	6	8	0	1			6	3	0	0	0	0	12.38
MILLER, STU	704	1694	105	103			1164	600	93	24	5	154	3.24
MIRABELLA, PAUL	156	316.1	11	23			163	161	31	3	1	0	4.92
MITCHELL, PAUL	125	621	32	39			277	191	95	11	4	1	4.45
MOELLER, RON	52	153	6	9			104	100	22	1	1	0	5.76
MOORE, RAY	365	1073	63	59			612	560	105	24	5	46	4.06
MOROGIELLO, DAN	22	37.2	0	1			15	10	0	0	0	1	2.39
MORRIS, JOHN	132	233	11	7			137	86	10	7	0	2	3.94
NARUM, BUSTER	98	397	14	27			220	177	56	9	2	0	4.44
NELSON, ROGER	135	636	29	32			371	190	77	20	7	4	3.06
NEWSOM, BOBO	600	3758	211	222			2082	1732	483	246	30	21	3.99
NIEDENFUER, TOM	295	424	29	28	136	130	340	136	0	0	0	63	2.76
O'CONNOR, JACK	80	248.2	13	14			128	127	27	6	1	0	4.99
O'DELL, BILLY	479	1816	105	100			1133	556	199	63	13	48	3.30
O'DONOGHUE, JOHN	256	751	39	55			377	260	96	13	4	10	4.07
OSTEEN, DARRELL	29	38	1	4			34	29	1	0	0	3	8.05
OVERMIRE, FRANK	266	1130	58	67			301	325	137	50	11	10	3.97
PACELLA, JOHN	69	180.1	4	10			111	120	21	0	0	2	5.84
PAGAN, DAVE	85	232	4	9			143	95	18	3	1	4	4.97
PAIGE, SATCHELL	179	476	28	31			290	183	26	7	4	32	3.29
PALICA, ERV	246	839	41	55			423	399	80	20	3	12	4.23
PALMER, JIM	558	3947.1	268	152			2212	1311	521	211	53	4	2.86
PAPPAS, MILT	520	3186	209	164			1728	858	465	129	43	4	3.40
PARROTT, MIKE	119	494	19	39			266	190	68	14	2	5	4.88
PENA, ORLANDO	427	1203	56	77			818	352	93	21	4	40	3.70
PHOEBUS, TOM	201	1030	56	52			725	489	149	29	11	6	3.33
PILLETTE, DUANE	188	904	38	66			305	391	119	34	4	2	4.40
PORTOCARRERO, A.	166	818	38	57			338	320	117	33	5	2	4.31
QUIRK, ART	14	48	3	2			30	26	8	1	0	0	5.25
RAMIREZ, ALLAN	11	57	4	4			20	30	10	1	0	0	3.47
REYNOLDS, BOB	140	254	14	16			167	82	2	0	0	21	3.15
RICHERT, PETE	429	1166	80	73			925	424	122	22	3	51	3.19
ROBERTS, ROBIN	676	4689	286	245			2357	902	609	305	45	25	3.40
ROGOVIN, SAUL	150	885	48	48			388	308	121	43	9	2	4.06
ROWE, KEN	26	45	2	1			19	14	0	0	0	1	3.60
SCHMIDT, DAVE	221	436.1	23	28	179	154	270	119	14	1	1	34	3.18
SCHMITZ, JOHNNY	366	1813	93	114			746	757	235	86	16	19	3.54
SCHNEIDER, JEFF	11	24	0	0			17	12	0	0	0	0	4.88
SCOTT, MICKEY	133	172	8	7			70	50	0	0	0	4	3.71
SEVERINSEN, AL	88	111	3	7			53	47	0	0	0	9	3.08
SHORT, BILL	73	131	5	11			71	64	6	3	1	3	4.74
SLEATER, LOU	131	301	12	18			152	172	21	7	1	5	4.69
SNELL, NATE	82	180.1	6	4	82	63	71	53	0	0	0	5	3.14
STANHOUSE, DON	294	760.2	38	54			408	455	66	11	2	64	3.83
STARRETTE, HERM	27	46	1	1			21	16	0	0	0	0	2.54

PLAYER	G	IP	W	L	R	ER	SO	BB	GS	CG	SHO	SV	ERA
STEPHENSON, EARL	54	113	4	5			50	49	8	1	0	1	3.58
STEWART, SAMMY	334	929.2	55	46	399	365	561	481	25	4	1	42	3.53
STOCK, WES	321	518	27	13			365	215	3	0	0	22	3.60
STODDARD, TIM	386	560.1	35	30	257	238	459	292	3	0	0	65	3.82
STONE, DEAN	215	687	29	39			380	373	85	19	5	12	4.47
STONE, STEVE	320	1789	107	93			1065	716	269	43	7	1	3.96
STUART, MARLIN	196	486	23	17			185	256	31	7	0	15	4.65
SWAGGERTY, BILL	30	78.2	4	3			25	27	8	0	0	0	4.58
TORREZ, MIKE	494	3042	185	160			1404	1371	458	117	15	0	3.96
TROUT, DIZZY	521	2726	170	161			1256	1046	322	158	28	35	3.23
TRUCKS, VIRGIL	517	2684	177	135			1534	1088	328	124	33	30	3.38
TURLEY, BOB	310	1711	101	85			1265	1068	237	78	24	12	3.65
UNDERWOOD, TOM	379	1586.1	86	87			948	662	203	35	6	18	3.89
VINEYARD, DAVE	19	54	2	5			50	27	6	1	0	0	4.17
WALKER, JERRY	190	747	37	44			326	341	90	16	4	13	4.36
WATT, EDDIE	411	660	38	36			462	254	13	1	0	80	2.90
WIDMAR, AL	114	389	13	30			143	176	42	12	1	5	5.21
WIGHT, BILL	347	1562	77	99			574	714	198	66	15	8	3.95
WILHELM, HOYT	1070	2253	143	122			1610	778	52	20	5	227	2.52
WILSON, JIM	257	1540	86	89			692	608	217	75	19	2	4.01
ZOLDAK, SAM	250	930	43	53			207	301	93	30	5	8	3.54
ZUVERINK, GEORGE	265	642	32	36			223	203	31	9	2	40	3.54

Batting Record & Index

PLAYER	G	AB	R	H	2B	3B	HR	RBI	SB	SLG	BB	SO	AVG
ABRAMS, CAL	567	1611	257	433	64	19	32	138	12	.392	304	290	.269
ADAIR, JERRY	1165	4019	378	1022	163	19	57	366	29	.347	208	499	.254
ADAMS, BOBBY	1281	4019	591	1082	188	49	37	303	67	.368	414	447	.269
ALTOBELLI, JOE	166	257	27	54	8	3	5	28	8	.323	23	42	.210
ANDERSON, MIKE	721	1490	159	367	67	11	28	134	8	.362	61	343	.246
APARICIO, LUIS	2599	10230	1335	2677	394	92	83	791	506	.343	736	742	.262
ARFT, HANK	300	906	116	229	46	13	13	118	8	.375	137	118	.253
AVILA, BOBBY	1300	4620	725	1296	185	35	80	467	78	.388	562	399	.281
AYALA, BENNY	425	865	114	217	42	1	38	145	2	.434	71	136	.251
BAILOR, BOB	955	2937	339	775	107	13	9	222	90	.325	187	165	.264
BAKER, FLOYD	874	2280	285	573	76	13	1	196	23	.297	382	165	.251
BAKER, FRANK W.	146	288	28	55	8	3	1	24	4	.250	40	60	.191
BARKER, RAY	192	318	34	68	16	1	10	44	1	.358	76	76	.214
BATTS, MATT	546	1605	163	432	95	11	26	219	6	.391	143	163	.269
BAUER, HANK	1544	5145	833	1424	229	57	164	703	50	.439	521	638	.277
BAYLOR, DON	2072	7546	1141	1982	350	28	315	1179	280	.442	726	966	.263
BELANGER, MARK	2016	5784	676	1316	175	33	20	389	167	.280	576	839	.228
BENIQUEZ, JUAN	1377	4338	581	1193	176	29	70	421	104	.377	325	507	.275
BERARDINO, JOHNNY	912	3028	334	755	167	23	36	387	23	.355	284	268	.249
BLAIR, PAUL	1946	6042	776	1513	282	55	134	620	171	.382	449	877	.250
BLEFARY, CURT	863	2489	340	583	78	15	101	324	16	.399	456	444	.234
BONILLA, JUAN	398	1391	139	359	46	9	6	96	7	.317	111	99	.258
BONNER, BOB	61	108	15	21	5	1	0	8	1	.259	4	16	.194
BOWENS, SAM	479	1287	141	287	48	6	45	143	25	.375	100	293	.233
BOYD, BOB	693	1936	253	567	81	23	19	175	9	.388	167	114	.293
BRANDT, JACKIE	1221	3895	540	1020	175	37	112	485	45	.412	351	574	.262
BREEDING, MARV	415	1268	154	317	50	5	7	92	19	.314	66	180	.250
BRIDEWESER, JIM	329	620	79	156	22	6	1	50	7	.310	63	79	.252
BROWN, DICK	636	1866	175	475	62	3	62	223	7	.380	117	356	.244
BROWN, LARRY	1129	3449	331	803	108	13	47	254	25	.313	317	414	.233
BUFORD, DON	1286	4553	718	1203	175	44	93	418	200	.379	672	575	.264
BUMBRY, AL	1496	5053	778	1422	220	52	54	402	254	.378	471	709	.281
BURKE, LEO	165	301	33	72	7	2	9	45	0	.365	21	79	.239
BURLESON, RICK	1284	4933	630	1358	242	22	48	435	72	.362	403	447	.275
BUSBY, JIM	1352	4250	541	1113	162	35	48	438	97	.350	310	439	.262
CABELL, ENOS	1688	5952	753	1647	263	56	60	596	238	.370	259	691	.277
CARRASQUEL, CHICO	1325	4644	568	1199	172	25	55	474	31	.342	491	467	.258
CARREON, CAMILO	354	986	113	260	43	4	11	114	1	.349	97	117	.264
CASTLEMAN, FOSTER	268	662	58	136	24	3	20	65	4	.341	35	99	.205
CAUSEY, WAYNE	1105	3244	357	819	130	26	35	295	12	.341	390	341	.252
CIMOLI, GINO	969	3054	370	808	133	48	44	321	21	.383	221	474	.265
CLARY, ELLIS	223	650	97	171	32	4	2	46	12	.323	114	74	.263
COAN, GIL	918	2877	384	731	98	44	39	278	83	.359	232	384	.254
COGGINS, RICH	342	1083	125	287	42	13	12	90	50	.361	72	79	.265
COLEMAN, RAY	559	1729	208	446	74	33	20	199	19	.374	148	158	.258
COREY, MARK	57	57	10	12	2	0	1	7	0	.298	7	13	.211
COURTNEY, CLINT	946	2796	260	750	126	17	38	313	3	.366	265	143	.268
COX, BILLY	1058	3712	470	974	174	32	66	351	42	.380	298	218	.262
CROWLEY, TERRY	865	1518	174	379	62	1	42	229	3	.375	221	181	.250
CRUZ, TODD	544	1526	133	336	58	6	34	154	9	.333	59	318	.220
DALRYMPLE, CLAY	1079	3042	243	710	98	23	55	327	6	.335	387	403	.233
DAUER, RICH	1140	3829	448	984	193	3	43	372	6	.343	297	219	.257
DAVANON, JERRY	262	499	73	117	21	5	3	50	18	.315	68	80	.234
DAVIS, TOMMY	1999	7223	811	2121	272	35	153	1052	136	.405	381	754	.294

PLAYER	G	AB	R	H	2B	3B	HR	RBI	SB	SLG	BB	SO	AVG
DELSING, JIM	822	2461	322	627	112	21	40	286	15	.366	299	251	.255
DEMAESTRI, JOE	1121	3441	322	813	114	23	49	281	15	.325	168	511	.236
DEMARS, BILLY	80	211	29	50	5	1	0	14	2	.270	16	16	.237
DEMPSEY, RICK	1419	3949	438	939	183	12	78	380	17	.349	466	576	.238
DENTE, SAM	745	2320	205	585	78	16	4	214	9	.305	167	96	.252
DIERING, CHUCK	752	1648	217	411	76	14	14	141	16	.338	237	250	.249
DROPO, WALT	1288	4124	478	1113	168	22	152	704	5	.432	328	582	.270
DUNCAN, DAVE	929	2885	274	617	79	4	109	341	5	.357	252	677	.214
DURHAM, JOE	93	202	25	38	8	0	5	20	5	.272		50	.188
DWYER, JIM	1043	2128	304	543	95	16	56	268	20	.394	299	295	.255
DYCK, JIM	330	983	139	242	52	5	26	114	4	.389	131	140	.246
DYKES, JIMMY	2282	8046	1108	2256	453	90	109	1071	70	.400	954	849	.280
EDWARDS, HANK	735	2191	285	613	116	41	51	276	4	.440	264	264	.280
ELLIOTT, BOB	1978	7141	1064	2061	383	94	170	1195	60	.440	967	604	.289
EPSTEIN, MIKE	907	2854	362	695	93	7	130	380	7	.424	448	645	.244
ESSEGIAN, CHUCK	404	1018	139	260	45	4	47	150	0	.446	97	233	.255
ETCHEBARREN, ANDY	948	2618	245	615	101	17	49	309	13	.343	246	529	.235
EVERS, HOOT	1142	3801	556	1055	187	41	98	565	45	.426	415	420	.278
FINIGAN, JIM	512	1600	195	422	74	17	19	168	8	.367	190	115	.264
FIORE, MIKE	254	556	75	126	18	1	13	50	5	.333	124	99	.227
FLOYD, BOBBY	214	425	40	93	18	1	0	26	3	.266	18	99	.219
FOILES, HANK	608	1455	171	353	59	10	46	166	3	.392	170	295	.243
FORD, DAN	1153	4163	598	1123	214	38	121	566	61	.427	303	722	.270
FRANCONA, TITO	1719	5121	650	1395	224	34	125	656	46	.403	544	694	.272
FRAZIER, JOE	217	282	31	68	15	2	10	45	2	.415	35	46	.241
FREED, ROGER	344	717	49	176	27	2	22	109	1	.381	95	166	.245
FREY, JIM						No major league statistics							
FRIDLEY, JIM	152	424	50	105	12	5	8	53	3	.356	35	83	.248
FRIEND, OWEN	208	598	69	136	24	5	13	76	2	.339	55	109	.227
FULLER, JIM	107	315	24	61	17	0	11	41	1	.352	59	130	.194
GAINES, JOE	362	771	104	186	25	9	21	95	14	.379	81	197	.241
GARDNER, BILLY	1034	3544	356	841	159	18	41	271	19	.327	246	439	.237
GENTILE, JIM	936	2922	434	759	113	6	179	549	7	.486	475	663	.260
GINSBERG, JOE	695	1716	168	414	59	8	20	182	7	.320	226	135	.241
GOLDSBERRY, GORDON	217	510	78	123	20	2	6	56	2	.343	80	66	.241
GOODMAN, BILLY	1623	5644	807	1691	299	44	19	591	37	.378	669	329	.300
GRAHAM, DAN	143	412	39	99	10	1	17	65	0	.393	27	72	.240
GREEN, GENE	408	1151	130	307	49	7	46	160	2	.441	89	185	.267
GREEN, LENNY	1136	2956	461	788	138	27	47	355	78	.379	368	604	.267
GRICH, BOB	2008	6890	1033	1833	320	47	224	864	104	.424	1087	1278	.266
GROSS, WAYNE	1102	3123	374	727	126	9	121	396	24	.395	481	495	.233
GROTH, JOHNNY	1248	3808	480	1064	197	31	60	486	19	.395	419	322	.279
GULLIVER, GLENN	73	192	29	39	10	0	1	7	0	.271	46	23	.203
GUTIERREZ, JACKIE	320	879	98	208	20	5	4	54	25	.284	31	114	.237
GUTTERIDGE, DON	1151	4202	586	1075	200	64	39	391	95	.362	309	440	.256
HALE, BOB	376	626	41	171	29	2	2	89	0	.335	26	51	.273
HAMRIC, BERT	10	9	0	1	0	0	0	0	0	.111	0	0	.111
HANEY, FRED	622	1977	338	544	66	21	8	228	50	.342	282	123	.275
HANEY, LARRY	480	919	68	198	30	1	12	73	3	.289	44	175	.215
HANSEN, RON	1384	4311	446	1007	156	17	106	501	5	.351	551	643	.234
HARLOW, LARRY	449	1094	159	271	48	8	12	72	26	.339	156	205	.248
HARPER, TOMMY	1810	6269	972	1609	256	36	146	567	408	.379	753	1080	.257
HATTON, GRADY	1312	4206	562	1068	166	33	91	533	42	.374	646	430	.254

HELD, WOODY	1390	4019	524	963	150	22	179	559	14	.421	509	944	.240
HEMSLEY, ROLLIE	1593	5047	562	1321	257	72	31	555	29	.360	257	395	.262
HENDRICKS, ELLIE	711	1888	205	415	66	7	62	230	1	.361	229	319	.220
HERNANDEZ, LEO	66	205	21	50	6	1	6	26	1	.371	12	21	.244
HERZOG, WHITEY	634	1614	213	414	60	20	25	172	13	.365	241	261	.257
HITCHCOCK, BILLY	703	2249	231	547	67	22	5	257	15	.299	205	230	.243
HORNSBY, ROGERS	2259	8173	1579	2930	541	169	301	1584	135	.577	1038	679	.358
HUNTER, BILLY	630	1875	166	410	58	18	16	144	23	.294	111	192	.219
JACKSON, LOU	34	47	7	10	2	1	1	7	0	.362	1	13	.213
JACKSON, REGGIE	2705	9528	1509	2510	449	48	548	1659	226	.493	1342	2500	.263
JACKSON, RON	926	2986	356	774	165	22	56	342	18	.385	213	329	.259
JOHNSON, BOB W.	874	2307	254	628	88	11	44	230	24	.377	156	291	.272
JOHNSON, DARRELL	134	320	24	75	6	1	2	28	1	.278	26	39	.234
JOHNSON, DAVE A.	14435	4797	564	1252	242	18	136	609	33	.404	559	675	.261
KELL, GEORGE	1795	6702	881	2054	385	50	78	870	51	.414	620	287	.306
KELLERT, FRANK	122	247	25	57	9	3	8	37	0	.389	26	36	.231
KELLY, H. PAT	1385	4338	620	1147	189	35	76	418	250	.377	588	768	.264
KENNEDY, BOB	1483	4624	514	1176	196	41	63	514	45	.355	364	443	.254
KENNEDY, TERRY	962	3373	347	916	177	10	82	477	3	.403	238	565	.272
KIRKLAND, WILLIE	1149	3494	443	837	134	29	148	509	52	.422	323	648	.240
KLAUS, BILLY	821	2513	357	626	106	15	40	250	14	.351	331	285	.249
KLUTTZ, CLYDE	656	1903	172	510	90	8	19	212	5	.354	132	119	.268
KNIGHT, RAY	1240	3967	410	1102	230	25	67	497	13	.399	284	459	.278
KOKOS, DICK	475	1558	239	410	82	9	59	223	15	.441	242	252	.263
KRENCHICKI, WAYNE	550	1063	107	283	44	5	15	124	7	.359	106	141	.266
KRESS, RED	1391	5087	691	1454	298	58	89	799	47	.420	474	453	.286
KRYHOSKI, DICK	569	1794	203	475	85	14	45	231	5	.403	119	163	.265
LACY, LEE	1436	4291	615	1240	194	39	84	430	182	.411	340	608	.289
LANDRITH, HOBIE	772	1929	179	450	69	5	34	203	5	.327	253	188	.233
LANDRUM, TITO	513	854	105	219	36	11	12	99	15	.367	71	160	.256
LAU, CHARLIE	527	1170	105	298	63	9	16	140	3	.365	109	150	.255
LENHARDT, DON	481	1481	192	401	64	9	61	239	6	.450	214	235	.271
LIPON, JOHNNY	758	2661	351	690	95	24	10	266	28	.324	347	152	.259
LOCKMAN, WHITEY	1666	5940	836	1658	222	49	114	563	43	.391	552	383	.279
LOLLAR, SHERMAN	1752	5351	623	1415	244	14	155	808	20	.402	671	453	.264
LONG, DALE	1013	3020	384	805	135	33	132	467	0	.464	353	460	.267
LOPEZ, CARLOS	237	500	61	130	24	1	12	54	23	.384	25	98	.260
LOWENSTEIN, JOHN	1356	3450	510	879	137	18	116	439	128	.406	444	594	.255
LUND, DON	281	753	91	181	36	8	15	86	5	.369	65	113	.240
LUTZ, JOE	14	36	7	6	0	1	0	2	0	.222	6	9	.167
LYNN, FRED	1537	5589	906	1632	336	40	241	926	64	.496	716	847	.292
MADDOX, ELLIOTT	1029	2843	360	742	121	16	18	234	60	.334	409	358	.261
MAJESKI, HANK	1069	3421	404	956	181	27	57	501	10	.398	299	260	.279
MANUSH, HEINIE	2009	7653	1287	2524	491	160	110	1173	114	.479	506	354	.330
MAPES, CLIFF	459	1193	199	289	55	13	38	172	8	.406	168	213	.242
MARSH, FREDDIE	465	1236	148	296	43	8	10	96	13	.311	125	171	.239
MARSHALL, JIM	410	852	111	206	24	7	29	106	5	.388	101	139	.242
MATCHICK, TOM	292	826	63	178	21	6	4	64	6	.270	39	148	.215
MAXWELL, CHARLIE	1133	3245	478	856	110	26	148	532	18	.451	484	545	.264
MAY, DAVE	1253	3670	462	920	130	20	96	422	60	.375	344	501	.251
MAY, LEE	2071	7609	959	2031	340	31	354	1244	39	.459	487	1570	.267
MELE, SAM	1046	3437	406	916	168	39	80	544	15	.408	311	342	.267
MICHAELS, CASS	1288	4367	508	1142	147	46	53	501	64	.353	566	406	.262
MIKSIS, EDDIE	1042	3053	383	722	95	17	44	228	52	.322	215	313	.236
MILLS, BUSTER	415	1379	200	396	62	19	14	163	24	.390	131	137	.287
MIRANDA, WILLIE	824	1914	176	423	50	14	6	132	13	.271	165	250	.221
MOLINARO, BOB	401	803	106	212	25	11	14	90	45	.375	65	57	.264
MORA, ANDRES	235	700	71	156	27	2	27	83	1	.383	31	149	.223
MORALES, JOSE	733	1305	126	375	68	6	26	207	0	.408	89	182	.287
MOSES, WALLY	2012	7356	1114	2138	435	110	89	679	174	.416	821	457	.291
MOSS, LES	824	2234	210	552	75	4	63	276	2	.369	282	316	.247
MOTTON, CURT	316	567	85	121	20	1	25	89	5	.384	86	116	.213

MURRAY, EDDIE	1499	5624	884	1679	296	20	275	1015	55	.505	709	769	.299
MURRAY, RAY	250	731	69	184	37	6	8	80	1	.352	55	67	.252
MUSER, TONY	663	1268	123	329	41	9	7	117	14	.323	95	138	.259
NELSON, BOB	79	122	11	25	2	2	0	11	0	.254	15	40	.205
NICHOLSON, DAVE	538	1419	184	301	32	12	61	179	6	.381	219	573	.212
NIEMAN, BOB	1113	3452	455	1018	180	32	125	544	10	.474	435	512	.295
NOLAN, JOE	621	1454	156	382	66	10	27	178	7	.378	164	183	.263
NORDBROOK, TIM	128	169	27	30	1	1	0	3	4	.195	25	26	.178
NORTHRUP, JIM	1392	4692	603	1254	218	42	153	610	39	.429	449	635	.267
O'MALLEY, TOM	316	937	88	238	37	5	9	95	2	.333	104	116	.254
O'NEILL, STEVE	1586	4795	448	1259	248	34	13	537	30	.337	592	283	.263
OATES, JOHNNY	593	1637	146	410	56	2	14	126	11	.313	141	149	.250
OLIVER, BOB	847	2914	293	745	102	19	94	419	17	.400	156	562	.256
ORSINO, JOHNNY	332	1014	114	252	44	5	40	123	3	.420	92	191	.249
PARDO, AL	34	75	3	10	1	0	0	1	0	.147	3	15	.133
PARIS, KELLY	68	149	14	33	6	0	0	8	8	.262	15	29	.221
PEARSON, ALBIE	988	3077	485	831	130	24	28	214	77	.355	477	195	.270
PELLAGRINI, EDDIE	563	1423	167	321	42	13	20	133	13	.316	128	201	.226
PHILLEY, DAVE	1904	6296	789	1700	276	72	84	729	102	.377	596	551	.270
PILARCIK, AL	668	1614	205	413	66	7	22	143	41	.346	185	150	.256
PINIELLA, LOU	1747	5867	651	1705	305	41	102	766	33	.409	368	541	.291
PISONI, JIM	103	189	26	40	3	3	6	20	0	.354	16	47	.212
POPE, DAVE	230	551	75	146	19	7	12	73	7	.390	40	113	.265
PORTER, J.W.	229	.544	58	124	22	1	8	62	4	.316	53	96	.228
POWELL, BOOG	2042	6681	889	1776	270	11	339	1187	20	.462	1001	1226	.266
POWERS, JOHNNY	151	215	26	42	7	2	6	14	0	.330	22	48	.195
PRIDDY, GERRY	1296	4720	612	1252	232	46	61	541	44	.373	624	639	.265
PYBURN, JIM	158	294	36	56	5	5	3	20	6	.272	34	56	.190
RAYFORD, FLOYD	370	994	107	244	43	1	36	114	4	.399	53	216	.245
RETTENMUND, MERV	1023	2555	393	693	114	16	66	329	68	.406	445	382	.271
RICE, DEL	1309	3826	342	908	177	20	79	441	2	.356	382	522	.237
RICHARDS, PAUL	523	1417	140	321	51	5	15	155	15	.301	157	149	.227
RIPKEN, CAL	830	3210	529	927	183	20	133	472	11	.483	313	417	.289
RIVERA, JIM	1171	3552	503	911	155	56	83	422	160	.402	365	523	.256
ROBINSON, BROOKS	2896	10654	1232	2848	482	68	268	1357	28	.401	860	989	.267
ROBINSON, EARL	170	421	63	113	20	5	12	44	7	.425	47	92	.268
ROBINSON, EDDIE	1314	4279	545	1145	171	24	172	723	10	.439	520	359	.268
ROBINSON, FRANK	2808	10006	1829	2943	528	72	586	1812	204	.537	1420	1532	.294
RODRIGUEZ, AURELIO	2017	6611	612	1570	287	46	124	648	35	.351	324	943	.237
ROENICKE, GARY	947	2443	331	611	122	4	111	375	16	.440	366	390	.250
ROJEK, STAN	522	1764	225	470	67	13	4	122	32	.326	152	100	.266
ROZNOVSKY, VIC	205	455	22	99	15	1	4	38	1	.281	32	83	.218
RUDOLPH, KEN	328	743	55	158	23	2	6	64	2	.273	52	121	.213
SAKATA, LENN	529	1210	154	272	44	3	23	100	30	.323	92	148	.225
SALMON, CHICO	658	1667	202	415	70	6	31	149	46	.354	89	233	.249
SANCHEZ, ORLANDO	74	110	11	24	3	2	0	12	1	.282	7	19	.218
SAVERINE, BOB	379	861	114	206	27	6	6	47	23	.305	73	149	.239
SCHULTZ, JOE	240	328	18	85	13	1	1	46	0	.314	37	21	.259
SHEETS, LARRY	233	682	88	185	26	1	36	112	2	.471	50	111	.271
SHELBY, JOHN	491	1354	188	325	50	13	30	135	52	.363	63	260	.240
SHETRONE, BARRY	60	112	12	23	2	1	1	7	3	.268	5	16	.205
SHOPAY, TOM	253	309	40	62	7	1	3	20	11	.259	26	51	.201
SIEBERN, NORM	1406	4481	662	1217	206	38	132	636	18	.423	708	749	.272
SIEVERS, ROY	1887	6387	945	1703	292	42	318	1147	14	.475	841	920	.267
SIMMONS, NELSON	84	281	35	73	13	0	10	36	2	.413	28	46	.260
SINGLETON, KEN	2082	7189	985	2029	317	25	246	1065	21	.436	1263	1246	.282
SISLER, GEORGE	2055	8267	1284	2812	425	164	102	1180	375	.468	472	327	.340
SKAGGS, DAVE	205	510	44	123	18	2	3	49	0	.302	51	76	.241
SMITH, AL	1517	5357	843	1458	258	46	164	676	67	.429	674	768	.272
SMITH, BILLY E.	370	1018	107	234	38	9	17	111	8	.335	96	189	.230
SMITH, HAL W.	879	2682	269	715	148	10	58	323	7	.394	196	361	.267

PLAYER	G	AB	R	H	2B	3B	HR	RBI	SB	SLG	BB	SO	AVG
SNYDER, RUSS	1365	3631	488	984	150	29	42	319	58	.363	294	438	.271
STALLER, GEORGE	21	85	14	23	1	3	3	12	1	.459	5	6	.271
STEFERO, JOHN	61	131	16	33	3	0	2	17	0	.321	19	27	.252
STEPHENS, GENE	964	1913	283	460	78	15	37	207	27	.355	233	322	.240
STEPHENS, VERN	1720	6497	1001	1859	307	42	247	1174	25	.460	692	685	.286
STILLMAN, ROYLE	89	155	19	33	7	1	3	15	2	.329	21	28	.213
STIRNWEISS, GEORGE	1028	3695	604	989	157	68	29	281	134	.371	541	447	.268
SWIFT, BOB	1001	2750	212	635	86	3	14	238	10	.280	323	233	.231
TASBY, WILLIE	583	1868	246	467	61	10	46	174	12	.367	201	327	.250
TAYLOR, JOE	119	297	34	74	16	1	9	31	0	.401	28	61	.249
TEMPLE, JOHNNY	1420	5218	720	1484	208	36	22	395	140	.351	648	338	.284
THOMAS, VALMY	252	626	56	144	20	3	12	60	2	.329	45	79	.230
THOMPSON, BOBBY	64	120	23	27	3	3	2	12	7	.350	9	26	.225
THOMPSON, HANK	933	3003	492	801	104	34	129	482	33	.453	493	337	.267
THRONEBERRY, MARV	480	1186	143	281	37	8	53	170	3	.416	130	295	.237
TRABER, JIM	75	233	31	59	7	0	13	46	0	.451	20	35	.253
TRIANDOS, GUS	1206	3907	389	954	147	6	167	608	1	.413	440	636	.244
UPTON, TOM	181	525	60	118	9	9	2	42	8	.288	65	67	.225
VALENTINE, FRED	533	1458	180	360	56	10	36	138	47	.373	156	228	.247
VAN GORDER, DAVE	162	389	26	84	12	1	2	37	1	.267	35	55	.216
VIRGIL, OSSIE	324	753	75	174	19	7	14	73	6	.331	34	91	.231
WAITKUS, EDDIE	1140	4254	528	1214	215	44	24	373	28	.374	372	204	.285
WARD, PETE	973	3060	345	776	136	17	98	427	20	.405	371	539	.254
WARWICK, CARL	530	1462	168	363	51	10	31	149	13	.360	127	241	.248
WASHINGTON, RON	461	1277	152	340	47	19	17	119	25	.373	55	212	.266
WEAVER, EARL					No major league statistics								
WERTZ, VIC	1862	6099	867	1692	289	42	266	1178	9	.469	828	841	.277
WESTLAKE, WALLY	958	3117	474	848	107	33	127	539	19	.450	317	453	.272
WIGGINS, ALAN	475	1702	279	450	54	16	4	92	201	.322	183	135	.264
WILLIAMS, DICK	1023	2959	358	768	157	12	70	331	12	.392	227	392	.260
WILLIAMS, EARL	889	3058	361	756	115	6	138	457	2	.424	298	574	.247
WOOD, KEN	342	995	110	223	52	7	34	143	1	.393	102	141	.224
WOODLING, GENE	1796	5587	830	1585	257	63	147	830	29	.431	920	477	.284
WRIGHT, TOM	341	685	75	175	28	11	6	99	1	.355	76	123	.255
YORK, RUDY	1603	5891	876	1621	291	52	277	1152	38	.483	791	867	.275
YOUNG, BOBBY	687	2447	244	609	68	28	15	137	18	.318	208	212	.249
YOUNG, MIKE	410	1258	181	323	56	5	54	177	11	.438	157	313	.257
ZARILLA, AL	1120	3535	507	975	186	43	61	456	33	.405	415	382	.276
ZUPO, FRANK	16	18	3	3	1	0	0	0	0	.222	2	6	.167